EDZELL GOLF CLUB
THE FIRST HUNDRED YEARS

The illustrations depicting James Braid and the Clubhouse (front cover), and Harry Vardon (back cover), are reproduced from original watercolours by Peter Davidson, who also created the overall cover design.

Painting of the course, presented to Edzell Golf Club
by the artist, Dr James Morrison, RSA, RSW, D. Univ.

EDZELL GOLF CLUB

THE FIRST HUNDRED YEARS

I. A. N. HENDERSON

FOREWORD BY LORD RAMSAY

EDZELL GOLF CLUB

IN ASSOCIATION WITH
JOHN DONALD PUBLISHERS LTD
EDINBURGH

ISBN 0 85976 407 9

A catalogue record for this book
is available from the British Library.

Typeset by ROM-Data Corporation Ltd, Falmouth, Cornwall
Printed in Great Britain by Arrowsmith Ltd., Bristol

Foreword by Lord Ramsay

This is not just the story of Edzell Golf Club; it is a fascinating piece of social history about Edzell and the people who live nearby. It starts with my great great uncle Charlie Ramsay and the Rev. Thomas Sturrock in the Victorian age and takes you to the present day, from a course with rough sheep-grazed fairways and no greens to the one we know now. The progress is relentless, if held up by the odd disaster or squabble, and even today changes are taking place.

After you have read this book, you can feast your mind on so many wonderful images. Railway trains puffing through from Brechin, horse-drawn mowers, the first match competition with Taylor, Braid, Herd and Vardon, the wildlife on the course and many other images leave a kaleidoscope of pictures in one's mind.

Then there is the course itself, from its original layout through all the changes to greens, bunkers, tees and fairways. The landmark moments such as opening the new clubhouse in 1925 and piping water to the greens in 1935 are all described, but so are many other less significant but equally fascinating incidents.

More than anything, this story is about people. From the founding fathers onwards, we read about men with a love of golf and their club: the captains, secretaries, treasurers, professionals, greenkeepers and committee men, all of whom over the years have put in many thousands of hours of work to give us what we now have. We, the ordinary members, owe them a great debt of gratitude, and still the work goes on.

We all have wonderful memories of golfing at Edzell. One incident remains in my mind. I was walking my dogs in Edzell wood and could see through the trees to the bank below the sixteenth green. An elderly member of the club was in the bunker and his companion above him on the green. After four or five efforts to get his ball up the bank onto the green, he looked round surreptitiously, saw the coast was clear, picked up the ball with a large handful of sand and threw it onto the green. Who can tell what the game of golf will do to honest men?

Finally, we must thank the author Mr I. A. N. Henderson for all the research and hard work he has put in to bring the history of Edzell Golf Club to life.

London, 1994

James Ramsay

v

Introduction to the Centenary History

As the last Captain of the first hundred years and the first of the second, we have had our perception of Edzell's place in the golfing scene particularly heightened. The more one is involved with the life and routine of Edzell Golf Club, the more one learns of its history and the better one appreciates just what we have to enjoy.

Our centenary coincides with that of nineteen other clubs in Scotland and many more around the world, as 1895 was the middle of a golfing boom such as we are in now. Few of those centenary clubs can claim to have played eighteen holes over the same land to such universal acclaim throughout their history, and few have been able to offer their members and visitors such quiet enjoyment in such scenic surroundings. The club is fortunate, still, to have a widespread membership drawn from Angus and the Mearns covering the whole spectrum of the community, which gives the ambience, the understatement and the casualness which is a delight to some members and infuriates others.

The French have a saying, 'Plus ça change, plus c'est la même chose'. That's Edzell! We commend I. A. N. Henderson's History of the Edzell Golf Club to you.

W. M. Low, Captain, 1993–5
J. E. Adams, Captain, 1995–

Acknowledgements

My thanks go to Jack Finlayson for his photographs of the course, to Peter Davidson for the cover, to Ian Cowie for proof-reading, and to all those people who loaned photographs for reproduction—with a special 'thank you' to Buffie for the photograph of her great-grandfather, the Rev. T.C. Sturrock.

Brechin, 1994   *I.A.N. Henderson*

Contents

Edzell Idyll

Underneath the Caterthuns
Where the dark West Water runs
And the breeze sighs, softly, sweetly, to the stream;
That's where Edzell golfers go
To restore the *status quo*
And recapture what they can of love's young dream.

But each Edzell Golf Club member
Should be cautioned to remember
That his forbears still predominate his game.
They took fields from Edzell Mains,
Built their course and then took pains
To put hazards where that member has to aim.

Then with undisguised contempt
They made one supreme attempt
To confound the simple golfer at his play.
Where the course was fairly open
They made sure the view was broken
By a colonnade of trees along the way.

How the Reverend T.C.S.
Could initiate such stress
And the Honble. C. M. Ramsay could condone
Such diversion from the truth
Is an uncontested proof
Of the claim that troubles never come alone.

Now your Edzell golfer's fate
Is to play his game and hate
Every flower and bush and tree and source of beauty.
It's a consequence of playing
Such a silly game and saying
'Keep your head down—watch the ball—that's now your duty'.

—I. A. N. Henderson, 1994

The Founding of a Golf Club

The history of a golf club can usually be written quite adequately on the back of an envelope. A date, a location, a name or two and you have it. There is not a great deal to be said about your average golf club. Edzell Golf Club is rather different. There is much to be said about Edzell Golf Club.

It was founded in 1895, and its present course was opened in 1896. The Hon. C. M. Ramsay was its first Captain—*ad hoc* in 1895, formally appointed in 1896—and its first Secretary and Treasurer was the Rev. Thomas C. Sturrock, Minister of Edzell. The first members of Committee were Captain Scott, Messrs. H. Gordon, T. Anderson, D. G. Shiell, James Duncan, John Duke and D. Arnot. These are the basic facts of the Club's history, but because of the basic facts of Edzell's history and the close relationship between club and village, there is a wealth of detail to be added.

The first official mention of golf in Edzell appears in the *Golfer's Guide* of 1888–89, where it lists Edzell Golf Club as having been 'instituted in 1887'. Of its institution and establishment there is no specific mention. The *Golfing Annual* of 1888 gives the Captain as David Nairn, the Secretary as John Murray, Union Bank of Scotland, Edzell, and lists the Members of Committee. The 'home green' is given as Edzell Muir and John Hunter is named as greenkeeper. From that it is clearly established that golf was played in Edzell prior to 1888, possibly started in 1887 and probably had those officials listed for 1888.

On the other hand, golf may have been played in Edzell for centuries before that—and most probably was. The game is on record as having been played in Scotland since the 15th Century when it was very much a game of the aristocracy and even royalty. The connection of golf with royalty in Scotland is well authenticated. Historians tell us that James IV played golf; James V was a notably good player; his daughter, Mary, Queen of Scots, enjoyed the odd game. Her son, James VI of Scotland and I of Great Britain and Ireland, was 'an indifferent player but an enthusiastic supporter'. That could put him in with the rest of us.

It was during the reign of James VII/I, in 1608, that the first golf club of all was founded, in England, at Blackheath, now the Royal Blackheath Golf Club. Who is to say that with all the royalty and aristocracy that frequented Edzell Castle over the centuries, golf on Edzell Muir wasn't the attraction? For golf was played on Edzell Muir long before it ever appeared in the *Golfer's Guide*. Golf and Edzell grew together.

By the end of the 19th century Edzell was known internationally as a holiday resort, particularly with Americans. The village had two large hotels, the Panmure Arms and the Star (now the Central) and a plethora of porter-and-ale houses and bed-and-board establishments. Prominent American industrialists would lease Gannochy Lodge and other local shooting lodges, whilst lesser lights rented houses in the village itself. Many Edzell folk retreated to huts at the bottom of the garden and let their houses for the season. Edzell supported a vastly increased population from May to October.

The attractions for holidaymakers to 19th century Edzell were access to the glens, shooting, fishing, tennis, bowling, good hotels with good cuisine and, from an early but undefined date, golf. By the last decade of the century Edzell was flourishing to the extent that local entrepreneurs were clamouring for more hotels to be built, the railway to be connected, but first, foremost and more essentially, a new golf course to be created.

There were many reasons for needing a new golf course in Edzell just then. The most obvious was that folk walking on the Muir were beginning to complain about being hit by golf balls. The old featheries weren't so bad but these new gutties were quite a different thing. It was no longer a laughing matter. Something was going to have to be done.

These folk walking on the Muir were not just the good burghers of Edzell stretching their legs. It was a custom and a tradition for everyone in Edzell to walk on the Muir. All the residents of the hotels and guest houses, the *beau monde*, used to promenade on the Muir after dinner. On fine summer evenings the company from the Panmure and the Star would rise from the dinner table and proceed, in full dress, to walk across the Muir and down the main street before retracing their steps to the Muir and their respective hotels. It was a diversion for the hotel guests, an entertainment for the locals and a source of tribulation for the Edzell golfers. Elegant ladies in ornate dresses squired by smart gentlemen in dinner suits (black tie), whilst a credit to Society, were no more than an added hazard on a golf course. The golfers, who had been flailing away there on the Muir as long as anyone could remember, were a positive danger to the visitors.

It was apparent to everyone in Edzell that something had to be done, and in due course something was done. The Hon. Charles Maule Ramsay, M.P., Member for the constituency, and the Rev. Thomas C. Sturrock, M.A., B.D., Minister in Edzell, put their heads together, worked out a few ideas and tipped off some of their golfing friends. The immediate result of their deliberations is recorded as the first entry in the minute book of the Edzell Golf Club, listed as 'Calling Public Meeting re proposed new Golf Course':

A Meeting of gentlemen interested in the acquisition of a new Golf Course for Edzell was held in the Public School there on the evening of Thursday, 17th October, 1895. The Rev. Thomas C. Sturrock, B.D., occupied the chair. It was the opinion of all present that a new Golf Course was a desideratum, the present course of the Muir being too small, and in the summertime when there are many visitors in the village, dangerous. It

The Hon. C. M. Ramsay, MP.

was also the general opinion that the most suitable place for a new course was the ground to the South of the village and West of the wood, forming part of the farm of Mains of Edzell. On the motion of Mr. J. Anderson, Westside, it was agreed to call a public meeting for the 30th October to consider the whole question.

Thomas C. Sturrock, Chairman

In due course, on 30 October, 1895, at 6.00 p.m. in the Schoolroom, Edzell, a second meeting was held. The Rev. T. C. Sturrock was called to the chair. The minute of that meeting continues:

The Chairman explained the steps which had been taken and which led to the calling of this meeting and explained that the ground referred to in the above Minute as suitable for a Golf Course could be had from Lord Dalhousie's Curators, who had already had it surveyed by Mr Bob Simpson of Carnoustie who had marked out a provisional course.

Rev. T. C. Sturrock, MA, BD.

There is a lot to be learned from these first minutes—a lot more than is actually recorded. They show, for example, the speed with which they operated in those days. From the meeting on 17 October, when the idea of a new club was first mooted, to the second meeting on the 30th—a mere thirteen days—they had agreed to find a new course, arranged the lease of the ground and had it inspected, surveyed and marked out by Bob Simpson. That shows how good committee men work. By the time the second meeting was held, the whole thing had been organised and arranged and all that remained for the committee to do was to approve the result. This they duly did.

Bob Simpson, Golf Course Architect

The employment of Bob Simpson to mark out the course was significant. It showed that only the best was going to be good enough for Edzell Golf Club. Bob Simpson was the top man of his day. He was born in Earlsferry in Fife in 1863 and was apprenticed to Forgan of St Andrews as a clubmaker. His first golfing success came in 1880 at the age of seventeen when he finished second to Jimmy Anderson in the Open Championship. In 1883 he was appointed professional at Carnoustie 'to act as clubmaker, supervise the course, assist the secretary on medal days and coach the Members'.

In addition to all these varied skills—which were required of all professionals at the time—Bob Simpson added a special interest of his own: the layout and construction of new golf courses. The late 19th century saw an eruption of interest in golf and a demand for new courses greater even than the present, world-wide, demands. Bob Simpson was quick to see the need for qualified course builders. He studied course construction and modification and set up as a consultant. By the time the Hon. Charles Ramsay and the Rev. T. C. Sturrock approached him, Bob Simpson was the top golf course architect of his day. Edzell was wise—and lucky—to get Bob Simpson.

The demands on Bob's services for course construction were so great that he took his two brothers, Archie and Jack, into partnership, and between them they developed the business. Their original shop, built in 1875, was a long low building on the east edge of the Dalhousie Golf Club's ground. When Bob died on 1 May 1923, he left £3,640, a fair sum at that time and a bit more than most of his contemporary pros. The business had obviously prospered. His eldest son, Robert S. Simpson, carried on the shop until his death in 1978, when a grandson took over. In 1984 the family sold the business.

Bob Simpson involved himself with every aspect of the game and its appurtenances. He was closely concerned in the development of several new types of club and ball. His career coincided with the period of rapid expansion of golf, when it grew rapidly from being a minority sport of the aristocracy to being a popular pastime of the majority. At the start of Bob's career, clubs were known by name, not number; balls were either tophatfuls of boiled feathers or spheroid blobs of gutta percha. Tees were little mounds of sand. There was a lot of experimentation being done and Bob Simpson did a lot of it.

Particularly he was instrumental in developing the 'bulger' to replace the

Patrick Chalmers, Aldbar.

'long-nose' and though the very names are recherchés nowadays, that was one of the major advances in club design, ever. The bulger was the forerunner of the modern short-headed driver and was developed by a number of different clubmakers. One, Henry Lamb, credited himself with inventing it and calling it the bulger. A less successful rival is on record as saying 'On the other hand, only a very sure player can keep balls straight with the bulger'. Maybe his one bulged a bit too much.

This feature of shared discovery is common to many inventions and it seems to have been particularly prevalent amongst the early golf pros. As the guttie replaced the featherie and the rubber-core replaced the guttie, numerous claimants were heard for each stage. When Dr Haskell of Ohio thought he had invented the wound rubber-cored ball and applied for a patent, he was dismissed on the grounds of 'parallel development' by the brothers David and Walter Hewitt. In 1895, the year he was commissioned to lay out Edzell Golf Course, Bob Simpson produced a revolutionary form of driver with a head made out of compressed paper. He got the idea from the building trade where compressed pulped paper was being tried out as a replacement for stone. Neither Bob nor the building trade made much from that idea but it shows that Robert Simpson was rather more than just a Carnoustie lad who could play golf.

In his time Bob Simpson of Carnoustie was famous and in later life he became a leading figure in Carnoustie's civic scene. He served two years on the Council and rose to be a bailie. His name is honoured in Carnoustie today but his most durable memorials are the golf courses he designed: At Balgownie for Royal Aberdeen; Ferntower at Crieff; Oban, Moffat, Linlithgow, Alyth, Blair Atholl and, the diamond in his diadem, Edzell.

John Smith, Greenkeeper

When he was invited to design Edzell and mark out the course, he took with him his assistant, John Smith, who subsequently built the course under the 'superintendence' of Bob Simpson. As the spadework was starting, the Hon. Ramsay and the Rev. Sturrock were racing ahead with their plans. The 'Provisional Committee' members were being hustled along to authorise things they might not always have fully comprehended. At one Prov. Com. meeting on 8 July 1896, in Edzell Public School, for example, before the first item on the agenda was taken, the members were asked to approve minutes of meetings on 17 and 30 October 1895, and 18 January and 27 January 1896. There were some pretty important decisions included amongst that lot. The Hon. and the Rev. were paragons of expeditious committee management.

Reference to the meeting back on 18 January 1896, one feels, shows how innocuously they managed to introduce even the most controversial matters and have them accepted. The minute reads as follows:

> The Honble C. M. Ramsay met the Committee on the proposed Golf Course. Mr. Ramsay, after a friendly discussion with the Committee agreed to give the ground necessary for a Golf Course on a five year lease, at a cost of £50 per ann. No rent to be charged for the first two years and entry to be had at once, one condition of the lease being that residenters in Edzell, though not members of the Club, have the privilege of playing over the course for a yearly sum to be agreed upon between the Club and Mr. Ramsay, and embodied in the Rules of the Club. Mr. Ramsay stated that the Club would not have the right of grazing till after Martinmas 1896.
> It was agreed to appoint a suitable Greenkeeper at once.
> Mr. Anderson and the Secretary were appointed to draft rules and submit them to a future meeting of the Committee.

There you have it. Edzell Golf Club, founded in 1895, finally ratified in 1896. The technical points of the lease, on rent, duration and grazing rights, were straightforward and accepted as offered. At a subsequent meeting, on 8 February, John Smith who had assisted Bob Simpson to lay out the course, was appointed greenkeeper.

John Smith was to be paid £1 per week and a house was to be provided. A letter from Dalhousie Estates dated 28 April 1896, offers to build the house at an estimated cost of £190 without outhouse or water supply. These were to cost £30 to £40 extra and it was proposed to let the house to the club at an annual rent of

£10. When it was eventually built—complete with shed and tap—the house was late in completion and John Smith applied for compensation. The Club awarded him £4 and set his new wage, with house, at 18 shillings. Over all, even with 2 shillings a week knocked off his wages, John was much better off with his house.

The other proviso of the lease was of more immediate interest. 'One condition of the lease being that residenters of Edzell though not members of the Club, have the privilege of playing over the course for a yearly sum to be agreed upon between the Club and Mr. Ramsay and embodied in the Rules of the Club'. That was a surprise to everybody and it immediately removed the only adverse criticism that had ever been levelled at the new club.

Adverse criticism there had been, voiced quietly and anonymously when the new golf club had first been mooted. 'Just one more attempt by the Brechin nobs' it was whispered 'to keep the Edzell peasants in their place.' It was feared—and suggested—that the joining fee and annual subscription for the new club would effectively cut out most of the existing Edzell Muir golfers. Undisguised class distinction was blamed.

It is an accusation that would be entirely unthinkable nowadays, of course, since the social revolution of the 20th century that has brought democracy to the near edge of anarchy and given us the myth of the egalitarian society, but in 1895 social division was absolute. One was a gentleman or one was not. The Edzell men who played their golf on the Muir were not. They were tailors, blacksmiths, shopkeepers and hackney horse hirers. Good men and true, certainly; worthy representatives of the yeoman stock of Scotland, undoubtedly; but not gentlemen. It was said at the time that it was just one more move to give golf back to the aristocracy. Then the Hon. Charles made his stipulation and confounded the critics.

By writing into the rules of Edzell Golf Club a declaration of intent to provide near-free golf to Edzell 'residenters', he silenced all critisicm. The new club could satisfy the social pretensions of its members as much as they wanted by charging gentlemen's fees, but the good burghers of Edzell could continue to enjoy their golf unhindered, for five bob a year. It was a magnanimous gesture by the Hon. Charles that pleased everyone. He gave a final reassurance to the original golfers when he didn't close down their old course on the Muir but left it for anyone who wanted to use it. Bits of it were still being played on for years after that.

Unfortunately for Edzell citizens, the growth of the village over the years, the vast changes in national economic conditions and the purchase of the golf course by the club, have rendered the Hon. Charles's perquisite invalid. Edzell folk now have a degree of precedence in joining Edzell Golf Club, but only at the full current fees.

Start of Play

The new course was first played over on Saturday, 21 March 1896. It was a beautiful, natural stretch of mature heath with hardly a tree in sight. The first tee was alongside Dunlappie Road, where the second tee is now, but nearer to the roadside, and the ground between tee and green was totally unspoiled. The fairways were grazed by unobtrusive sheep, and the course was a paragon for its day. The Hon. Charles Ramsay and the Rev. Thomas C. Sturrock were congratulated and thanked by all. It is interesting to note that the names of David Nairn, the captain, and John Murray, the secretary, of the previous Edzell Golf Club, do not appear as members of the new.

Edzell was now well set to cater for the tourists on whom it depended. The Panmure Hotel and the Star had now been joined by the Edzell Hotel (now the Glenesk). The monumental Inglis Memorial Hall with its baroque architecture, free library and stained-glass windows was now attracting visitors in its own right. In 1896 the Brechin–Edzell Railway started its passenger service. There had been a bit of a hold-up with the railway when the line collapsed into a hole beside Trinity Muir. The engineers had apparently been unaware that they had laid their line over an old lime quarry. As the name of the place is Limefield and lime had been dug out of it for a century before that, one feels that maybe they should just have had some hint of it. When the passenger trains did run in 1896, they brought staggering numbers of visitors. For the fireworks display by Messrs Brock at the opening of the Inglis Memorial Hall, a special train left Brechin at 8.30 'by which nearly one thousand people of all classes travelled to witness the display.' Note the continual reference to 'class' in those days.

Excursion trains ran regularly from Dundee, Arbroath, Carnoustie, Forfar and Aberdeen and they brought ever increasing trainloads. In the men's bar of Edzell Golf Club today, there is a photograph on the wall showing a railway poster at Zagazig railway station in Egypt taken in 1908 advertising the glories of Edzell and its golf course. By the 1920s, on a Saturday in summer, one train would disgorge four hundred adults and one-hundred-and-fifty children: one train, mark you! These are the figures that show us the importance of Edzell as a holiday resort in its heyday.

The Matter of the Greens

Now that the golf course was open and played over regularly, the compliments started to come in, and, golfers being golfers then as now, so did the complaints. The first recorded complaints about Edzell Golf Course were about its greens: There weren't any. Any golf course worth its subscription in 1896 was providing turfed greens, and what about Edzell? What was John Smith doing for his near pound a week if he hadn't even turfed the greens? How, it was further asked, could anyone be expected to putt on the unshorn heath that was all that Edzell offered? One elderly stalwart—a five-shilling man—was heard to remark that he saw no benefit at all in leaving their perfectly good course on the Muir to come down to this windswept wasteland they had hacked out of Mains of Edzell's sheep pasture. He felt, personally, that it signalled the end of golf as he knew it.

To one such malcontent—a full member—the Rev. Thomas Sturrock made reply. Had the member not noted the decision to turf the greens taken at the meeting of 17 March 1896? Was the member not aware that, between that date and that of the meeting on 2 May 1896, the ninth and twelfth greens had in fact been turfed? That it was only because the season was so far advanced and there were so many other things to be done that the turfing of the remaining greens had been held over to the end of the season?

These revealing exchanges are recalled because they indicate clearly the start of a tradition that has been rigorously maintained in Edzell Golf Club to this day. The Infallibility of Edzell Golf Club secretaries. Over the years since, Edzell Golf Club secretaries have meticulously followed the lead of the Rev. Thomas Sturrock and clobbered dissenting members with the minute book. The book itself is studded with gems of illuminating reportage in illustration of that fact. He is a brave man who presumes to question the ukase of the Edzell Golf Club Secretary, ever.

With the matter of the greens settled to the secretary's satisfaction, the next murmur from the members was that they needed something to play for—some trophy or other. On 2 May 1896, the secretary intimated that Mr Henry Inglis of London had donated two medals, one gold and one silver, for club competition. These were first played for on Saturday, 6 June, when the Gold was won by J. Caithness with a score of 103–15 = 88, and the Silver by J. Duncan with 88 + 1 = 89. The Silver was subsequently played for as a monthly medal. The scores show that a sophisticated handicapping system was already in operation, a fifteen

The Ramsay Cup, 1898. Presented by the Hon. C. M. Ramsay.

handicapper taking the Gold from a plus-one man.

Give or take the odd bit of treachery from the greens, the course was now giving general satisfaction—its scenic beauties were much lauded in the local press—but there were still criticisms. The Hon. Charles himself was one of the most critical. His first suggestion was that they needed special rules for Edzell Golf Course and special rules he drew up under 'Special Rules for Course' on 21 May 1898;

1. A ball out of bounds in growing grain or green crop must be considered a lost ball and lost hole.
2. A ball on the railway or in the woods must be played as it lies or given up.
3. A player sending his ball into the river will lose stroke and distance.
4. A ball can be lifted from a rabbit scrape without penalty.

A glance at Special Rule No. 2 makes one wonder just how much authority the Club had over the railway. It could order trains to be run as required, certainly, but could they order trains to be stopped for shots to be played? It surely called for a very 'special rule' if they couldn't!

The Turn of the Century

The year 1898–99 was a busy one in the Club's history. The Rev. T. C. Sturrock resigned as secretary and treasurer owing to 'pressure of work'. No doubt some of his parishioners had been asking just how he managed to fit everything in. J. Anderson of Westside resigned as green convener, and, at the start of 1899, John Smith was sacked. John Smith, the man who had built the course 'under the superintendence of Bob Simpson' summarily dismissed with but one month's notice! There must have been a power of intrigue behind that decision. In his place, Alex Robertson of Forfar was appointed to be the quaintly titled 'Custodian of the Green'.

The Club survived these various vicissitudes and emerged the stronger for the experience. The Rev. Thomas Sturrock was replaced by two men, James Duncan and David Shiell, as joint secretary/treasurers. Alex Robertson gave such good service that they immediately raised his wages to a pound a week and allowed him to employ his son as assistant at a wage of 12 shillings a week 'so long as is necessary'. The Hon. Ramsay's suggestions for improving the course were partly implemented. A new hole was added to the west side of the course, one taken off the east side, and the eighteenth hole was extended. Further proposed alterations were held over 'for the time being'. In other words, the committee didn't mind giving the Hon. a bit of his own way but they weren't going to be ordered around even by the Hon. Ramsay. In any case, the Boer War was being fought just then, and even in Edzell, golf had to take second place. In October 1900 the Club agreed that 'Members of the Club serving with the imperial forces in South Africa be exempted from their subscriptions during their absence.'

Whilst the Boer War postponed any actual reshaping of the course, it did not stop the members from expressing their various views on the need for change. On 2 July 1902, the secretary wrote to Captain Stuart 'warning him that he must keep to the course prescribed by the Green committee'. The Captain's exact route round the course is not defined but he was obviously prematurely implementing some of the proposed improvements. He accepted the reprimand without reply, as a good soldier should, and leaves us wondering.

The Boer War ended with the peace treaty of 31 May 1902, and with the amazing speed that affairs were conducted in those days, by the 7 June, Edzell was arranging to hold a professional golfers' tournament. The dates were provisionally fixed for 28, 29 and 30 August: less than three months away. It certainly couldn't be done today. It was done in 1902. The minute of 7 June says:

> It was suggested and approved that the competition last for three days. The first to be 36 holes by strokes and the best eight to compete in a match competition on the second and third days. Eight in the forenoon of the second day, four in the afternoon of the same day and the final of 36 holes upon the third day. It was resolved to try to raise £120 as prize money.

Once the initial decisions had been made the work went ahead immediately. Advertisements were placed in all the national newspapers, trains were ordered to run from Dundee and Montrose to connect with Glasgow, Edinburgh and Aberdeen trains, and so much work was required on the course that Alex Robertson's wages were increased to 22 shillings a week, *nemine contra dicente*. This was to be the biggest thing of its kind, and an extract from the minute of 18 June shows just how important it was:

> It was agreed to write to Taylor, Braid, Herd and Vardon asking them if the dates would suit them and offering to pay their return Railway fares from their home green to Edzell. The Secretary was instructed to draw up a circular to be sent to the Secretaries of those clubs which employ prominent professionals. In the event of any of those Professionals being unable to come, the Secretary was empowered to pay the expenses of any of the English Professionals they might select, but not more than four.

The Edzell Professional Golf Tournament of 1902

Taylor, Braid, Herd and Vardon. Substitute Faldo, Ballesteros, Nicklaus and Watson and you might have some idea of the magnitude of the Edzell Professional Golf Tournament of 1902. They all attended and competed having first, formally, written their polite acceptance letters to the secretary, and the whole tournament was a huge success. At the next committee meeting the Hon. Ramsay was able to report that 'one of the professionals to whom he had spoken had said that they had never taken part in a competition in which the comfort of professional golfers had been so well looked after. Mr Adamson seconded, remarking that there had not been the slightest hitch in any of the arrangements.'

It was this tournament that finally established Edzell Golf Club in the top rank of golf clubs. Every leading professional golfer in Britain was there, including the top Frenchman, Arnaud Massey. Of the big four, Braid, Vardon and Herd made it through to the semi-finals along with J. White. In the semis, Vardon beat Braid and Herd beat White, setting up a Vardon–Herd final. In his semi-final, Harry Vardon set a record 67 for Edzell Golf Course and a collection was taken up to mark the achievement. His pay-off for the record was £9. 12 shillings. The 36-hole final between Vardon (Ganton) and Herd (Huddersfield) ended with Vardon the winner by one hole. He won £25 to add to his £9. 12 shillings. It is on record that professional golfers are paid more than that at the present day.

With the golf club now fully functional and accredited, the hotels booked out every summer and the railway disgorging hundreds of day trippers at weekends, Edzell was now a major tourist venue. In 1896 the *Brechin Advertiser* had carried an article by a Miss Jeannie M. Laing in which she stated, after having described Edzell in purple prose: 'The inhabitants of Brechin, which in this case includes Edzell, are well and favourably known for kindness of heart, unstinted hospitality and charming courtesy of manner, qualities which, added to the natural amenities of the district, have made them the attraction they are to the fashionable tourist and sportsman.' Whilst one is bound to query the validity of the lady's first subordinate clause, one accepts the simple truth of her premise. The Edzell folk are braw folk—hert o' corn. By 1902 the 'attraction to the fashionable tourist and sportsman' was so great that the *Brechin Advertiser* carried column inches listing the titles, ranks and names of all the visitors in the hotels, guest-houses and rented properties in Edzell. The 'Brechiner' served as a combined court circular and *Almanach de Gotha*. Indian Maharajas, Scandinavian royalty and American

W. Shaw Adamson.

millionaires rented shooting lodges in the district and patronised Edzell Golf Club. David Wilson, club member and Edzell blacksmith, worked as a hallboy for John Pierpont Morgan at Gannochy Lodge when he first left school. Dave will tell you all about the great days.

These were the members who helped mould Edzell Golf Club. The Earl of Dalhousie was President, W. Shaw Adamson of Careston Castle was Captain, the committee was made up of local lawyers, bankers, landowners and notables, but the body of the club has always been nourished by the lifeblood of its ordinary members. One mentions that, of course, for purely practical purposes—no hint of social superiority is inferred. Social eminence is an incidental element. It is the practical advantage of having influential members that has been of constant and lasting benefit.

Take, for example, the matter of the greens. When the arguments about the state of the greens were at their most heated, one of the rank-and-file members quietly remarked that, if it would help, he would donate enough money to cover the cost of any work needed to put them right. All argument ceased forthwith. The greens were subsequently renovated to the club's entire satisfaction at the expense of that member. He was Sir Everard Hambro, K.C.V.O., Member of Edzell Golf Club, and incidentally, Chairman of Hambro's Bank.

At that same meeting, another ordinary member chipped in to say that his other club, Sunningdale, was having similar problems with their greens. He then arranged for the Sunningdale staff to advise Edzell on the controlled use of moss litter: Sunningdale, mark you!

A further example came in 1903 when the club approached the railway company about the possibility of building a footbridge beside the thirteenth green (now the fourteenth). Without waiting for further discussion the railway company built the bridge and sent in a bill for £90. With most golf clubs that would have been that, but Edzell consulted a bevy of its lawyer-members and met the charge head on. Edzell Golf Club then informed the railway company that they, the railway company, had built the bridge without permission from the landlord or from the club. Edzell Golf Club, therefore, disclaimed all responsibility for the railway company's recently erected bridge. A compromise was hastily arranged whereby the railway withdrew its cost of £90 and Edzell Golf Club agreed to pay £6 per annum to help the railway maintain its handsome new trellis-work structure. A clear victory for the club!

It is probable that the railway company had failed to notice that the ground in question was owned by the Earl of Dalhousie, President of Edzell Golf Club, that the lawyer who stated the club's case was one D. G. Shiell, Secretary of Edzell Golf Club, and that a considerable *tranche* of the railway company's shares was held by assorted members of Edzell Golf Club. It's a wonder they even agreed to pay the £6.

It was the same D. G. Shiell, the secretary, who stepped off the Brechin train in Edzell station one fine May morning in 1909, carrying his bag of clubs and a half-load of worry. The club and D. G. were facing another problem. Here he was, heading for the course and a needle match with Percy Gordon, and he knew

On the 17th green (now the 1st), 1904.

that the club was hard pushed to find enough caddies. Playing a round of golf without a caddie was rather more than your Edzell member was prepared to endure in 1909. Sand tees had to be built, clubs cleaned for every shot, and medicinal flasks of barley-essence carried at the ready.

Girl Caddies

As he came down the platform that morning, heading for the Glenesk Hotel, D. G. Shiell met George Kerr, one of the railway company employees. D. G. knew George Kerr well from his regular use of the railway and he had a flash of inspiration and came up with an idea: 'I say, George,' says D. G. 'You're a family man—what about sending one of your sons down to the Glenesk to caddy for us?' Now George Kerr was, indeed, a family man. He and Mrs Kerr had nine of a family but only the youngest three were boys: too young for caddying. Fortunately George also had a flash of inspiration and came up with an idea:

'And what's wrong with girls?' says he.

'Oh, nothing, nothing at all, I suppose', says D. G. 'Would they care to have a go, do you think?'

'What time do you want them on the tee, Mr Shiell?' said George. And his two daughters, Alice and Agnes, reported for duty at 1.00 p.m. that day and started a tradition of girl caddies in Edzell Golf Club that lasted until caddy-cars displaced the species.

These are the facts that make Edzell Golf Club just that wee bit different from other golf clubs, and Edzell is proud of them. There are suave and elegant ladies hosting bridge parties in Edzell today who earned their pocket money in the 1930s, washing mashie-niblicks in the Wishop Burn for an extra threepence— after they had caddied for a shilling. Tell that to Fanny Sunesson.

The employment of girl caddies became a feature of Edzell Golf Club, and by the time the caddy-car took over there were always about twelve to fourteen young Edzell lassies on the caddy list. They were a feature of the club. Only occasionally did teensy little errors occur. Like the one when Alice Kerr's niece, Isobel Kerr, reported for her first stint as a caddy in 1933.

Isobel arrived, shining clean and wearing her beret as instructed. She built a neat little pyramid of a sand tee, proffered the driver graciously to her golfer, J. P. Gellatly, and stood rigidly still whilst he drove. Only when the ball was bounding down the fairway did Isobel put a foot wrong. She went scuddin' down the fairway after the ball to bring it back. They had forgotten to tell her the finer points of the game. Don't tell that to Fanny Sunesson.

It was shortly after that, that sand tees went and were replaced by bone or ivory pegs which usually had tassels attached to limit their flight and assist recovery. Mrs Ward (née Kerr) of Edzell showed me a braw pair that she used when she was at the caddying. I think the R. & A. could use them in their museum now.

Back to 1909 the minutes show how rigorously the members kept their committee on its toes. Ever since 1900 the club had paid the Glenesk Hotel £10 a year for the use of their billiard room as a clubroom. Over the next few years there were murmurs in the ranks about the need for a proper clubhouse. By 1911 the matter had been raised several times, to no avail. At the April general meeting of 1912, Mr J. B. Don of Maulesden was appointed *ad hoc* chairman and after the routine matters had been attended to, up spake Mr J. B. Don, and:

> The Chairman commented on the neglect of the Committee to lay before the Meeting a Report as to the advisability of a Club House in terms of the motion carried at the last General Meeting and stated that he considered that the Members had not been courteously treated by the Committee and he, with the approval of the Meeting, instructed to be noted in the Minutes the Meeting's disapproval of the Committee's conduct.

Thereafter, Mr T. C. Anderson moved that the new committee be asked to take up the question of a club house and present a report, etc., at a special meeting of the members to be called before the end of June. This motion was seconded by Mr Monro Scott and carried unanimously. A vote of thanks to the chairman terminated the proceedings, with, one imagines, a warm feeling of satisfaction for the members.

The fact that it was subsequently agreed not to go ahead with the building of a clubhouse until long after, was irrelevant. The Committee had been ticked off and told to get on with the job. The members were satisfied.

Sunday Golf

The club was now into its eighteenth year, well established and accepted as a prime attraction for the Edzell folk and visitors alike. It would appear that the foresight of its founder members had been fully justified. All seemed well set for the members, visitors and residents who shared the pristine facilities in their dedicated pursuit of health, happiness and the wee white ba'. Indeed all would have been well set for them if it had not been for the inevitable conflict of God and Mammon over the matter of Sunday golf.

Sunday golf was something of a novelty in 1913, and Edzell Golf Club had allowed Sunday golf since 1896. Edzell, the village, was divided—aye, fragmented—on the issue. Men, women and golfers banded themselves together into groups to fight the cause. Sunday golf or no Sunday golf. The village was split, the club was split, marriages and Saturday forenoon foursomes were split as Edzell pulsated to the throb of conflict.

It is hard for us now to assess the intensity of that conflict. These were the days before two World Wars and Channel Four had eroded the power of the Church to control its adherents. Hellfire and damnation were still accepted as reasonable reward for even the simplest sins, and playing golf on Sundays was a sin of complex proportion. It encompassed sacrilege, apostasy and, worst of all, enjoying yourself.

There was even a compounding of these sins in that the Rev. T. C. Sturrock, a minister of the gospel, was secretary and founding father of Edzell Golf Club. Now we see what had prompted him to resign back in 1898 'due to pressure of business'. For years the Rev. T. had been suffering a power of abuse from at least one half of his parishioners. How could he, a minister in holy orders, allow Sunday golf? It was all very well for him to resign as Secretary because of Sunday golf but how could he then remain a member of a club that allowed Sunday golf? There is no doubt that the Rev. T. C. Sturrock was caught by the seat of his breeks on at least one horn of a dilemma, for the Rev. Tom liked his golf.

On 4 September 1913, a petition to Edzell Golf Club was composed and drawn up for submission. It was a paragon of its kind, deferential in approach, complimentary in address and scathing in condemnation. It thanked the golf club for its contribution to the material prosperity of Edzell generally and recognised the benefit of near-free golf for Edzell golfers. It was a model of copperplate calligraphy and is here in full:

To the Members of the Edzell Golf Club.   Edzell, 4th September, 1913.

My Lords and Gentlemen,

We, the undersigned, being householders in the village of Edzell, venture most respectfully to approach you in regard to the question of Sunday Golf. In doing so we do not suggest that we have in any way, a right to interfere with the administration of the affairs of the Edzell Golf Club; and we would take this opportunity of expressing our hearty recognition of the important part the Golf Course plays in furthering the material prosperity of the community and our cordial appreciation of the valuable privileges we ourselves enjoy in the use of the Course. At the same time we feel that the question of the observance of the Sunday has aspects which make it one that concerns the community, and we have reason to believe that everything that tends to rob that day of its distinctive character by putting it on a level with the other days of the week is very much against the moral welfare of the community, and, in particular, exercises an injurious influence upon the young.

It has always been to us a matter of genuine regret that play is permitted on the Edzell Course on Sunday, and that regret has been deepened by the fact that this year the practice has shown a tendency to increase.

We, therefore, humbly submit for your consideration that Sunday Golf is opposed to the prevailing sentiment in Scotland; that it is not permitted on any other Course in Forfarshire or in the neighbouring Counties; that we feel so strong an objection to the practice that we have been constrained to approach you in this way, and that we cherish the hope that you may see your way to close the Course altogether for play on Sunday.

We are,
My Lords and Gentlemen,
Yours respectfully.

There follows three columns of signatures of Edzell residents; 103 in all, comprised of 67 men and 36 women. No doubt they could have had more, but the space on the paper was all used up. The significant fact for the Rev. T. C. Sturrock is that his name led all the rest. Top line, middle row. There is no doubt that the Rev. was opposed to Sunday golf. He couldn't have been otherwise. He had already raised the matter back in 1906 and been voted out with only the conciliatory concession that no caddies could be employed on Sundays. Edzell knew that T. C. stood out against Sunday golf, but a lot of Edzell folk thought that he should resign from the golf club altogether. The petition made his position clear to all.

When the neatly folded missive, labelled 'Letter from Householders in Edzell to the Members of the Edzell Golf Club, 4th September, 1913', was handed in, it was taken along by the secretary to the annual meeting on 13 September. After a Motion: an Amendment: a vote called on the Amendment taken as the Substantive Motion, it was decided that the Petition 'be not read to the meeting'. That was it. A photo copy of the petition now hangs in the Men's Bar and not a lot of folk ever look at it.

In a general sense, a golf club is not a body that can be described as precipitate. Golf clubs tend to take their time. Ideas, suggestions and complaints can ricochet around golf clubs for years before any action need be considered. A bicycle rack suggested to Edzell Golf Club in 1908 was erected in 1971. It is in the nature of the game itself. Your golfer is used to expending maximum energy to propel an insignificant load over a series of relatively short distances, using totally ineffectual implements, to his dubious enjoyment. It is little wonder that golfers procrastinate. Golfers are not rational thinkers. To a golfer a one-inch putt equals a 250-yard drive.

The Story of the Clubhouse

Thus it is that the story of Edzell Golf Club's clubhouse is disjointed and of protracted interest. It started when the club started. Straightaway the members needed somewhere to meet and change and store their clubs and sit down afterwards and tell other members of their misfortunes. At first they used the Star, the Panmure and the Glenesk. In 1900 they rented the billiard room in the Glenesk. In 1912 they had that little internal schism between members and committee when all the old arguments started up again and the matter just rumbled on.

The billiard room in the Glenesk served well as a club room. For ten pounds a year the golfers had exclusive use of it when required, and it provided a changing room with lockers and a choice of refreshment rooms. The main drawback was the lack of a private committee room for meetings. The club committee and the various sub-committees were peripatetic and forced to meet wherever they could find an available space. Members who were solicitors, bankers and teachers made available their various offices, banks, and schools as required in Edzell and Brechin, but there was a constant murmur of complaint. They needed their own premises.

The War of 1914–18 had held up all action on the matter, but immediately after the war the question was raised again. The general opinion was that they should buy a house somewhere near the first tee and convert it into a clubhouse. This had been proposed and discussed long before the war, but most of the members had preferred the use of the Glenesk at that time. When the suggestion was made again in 1919, two houses were on the market in reasonable proximity to the course, one in the High Street and one in Dunlappie Road. The Dunlappie Road house, 'Strathairlie', was just across the road from the railway station and the first tee, so it became the obvious choice. Members were circularised and asked for opinions and financial backing and, surprisingly, they voted it down. It was a close-run thing but the balance was just in favour of a new clubhouse. The strong Strathairlie faction then switched its allegiance to the new clubhouse group and the thing became practically unanimous. On 20 September 1923, in the Clydesdale Bank Buildings in Brechin, the Committee of the Edzell Golf Club finally drew up plans for the erection of the first Edzell Golf Club Clubhouse.

No doubt the committee felt better for having made the decision and, possibly, the excitement of it all went to their heads a bit, for their next proposal was to re-shape the whole course. All these years that the Hon. Ramsay had been carping away about the state of the course seemed to have taken effect at last. It was now suggested that the whole course should be redesigned ready for the opening of the new clubhouse.

There was one very sound reason for reorganising the course: the siting of the new clubhouse. This decision caused one of the biggest divisions the club has ever known. When the Strathairlie battle had been fought, the cost of the house and alterations necessary to make it into a clubhouse had been estimated at £1,650. In response to the Circular asking for support and financial backing, only 19 members had agreed to take 33 £5 shares, so the scheme fell through. This was in 1920, and now in 1923 the club was going to need £3,000. Add to that the arguments raging about whether or not the club should build a footbridge over the railway at the station and one can gauge the complexity of the whole thing. In essence, there were three main points to be decided. One; the siting of the new clubhouse. Two; the siting of the first tee in relation to the new Club house with the consequent alteration to the golf course. Three; the need/desirability of a footbridge over the railway to improve access to and from the new clubhouse.

Each of these points was prone to unlimited opinion and discussion and unlimited opinion and discussion ensued. It provided the clash o' the country for months. Sunday golf sank over the horizon. The tarring of the Gassie Brae and the renovation of the Castle box-hedge garden faded into the background. Edzell rang to golf club chimes. The only redeeming feature for the committee was that, unlike the Sunday-golf row, they were spared hellfire and damnation. Everything else they got.

When one considers the thought processes required of a golfer, it is not entirely surprising that Edzell Golf Club was meticulous in its preparation—it is little wonder that any club composed entirely of golfers should have difficulty in arriving at a decision. In practising his arcane art, your golfer has habitually to concern himself with a complex series of variable factors, any one of which may nullify his every effort. His feet, knees, hips, shoulders, head and eyes must be maintained in perfect alignment to the ball. His stance must be kept parallel to the line of flight, his swing smooth and unhurried through the desired arc. How then can such a man be expected to make snap decisions on club policies? It takes time. The amazing part of it all is the speed with which Edzell Golf Club did act once its decisions had been made.

In this case every member of the club was first sent a circular on 6 November 1923, asking for agreement to raise £2,000 by members' loans in units or multiples of £10. They had the balance of £1,000 in the kitty. Having secured sufficient promises of funds, the next stage was to approach the members again, on 21 January 1924, offering a choice of three schemes involving two proposed Club House sites and the choice of a footbridge over the railway or not. These offers were:

Scheme 1:   Do you prefer Site 'M' with the erection of a footbridge on the Railway Company's terms?
Scheme 2:   Do you prefer Site 'S' with the erection of a footbridge on the said terms?
Scheme 3:   Do you prefer the Course to remain as it is and no footbridge to be erected. Under this Scheme the Club House would be erected on site 'S' and would entail a walk from the Club House to the 1st Tee in Dunlappie Road.

Sketches were annexed showing the various possible permutations of all the variables, and Edzell's heid dirled wi' the claik. Every detail was explained on the circular and the choice restricted to Schemes 1, 2, or 3.

At the meeting of 1 February 1924, in the Clydesdale Bank Buildings in Brechin, the envelopes containing the voting slips were opened. From a membership of just over a hundred the result was:

Scheme 1: 27 votes
Scheme 2: 18 votes
Scheme 3: 46 votes

That decision put the clubhouse where it is today.

The consequent upheaval to the club was massive but the committee kept the best interests of the members always to the fore. Instead of charging ahead and signing up a course-builder at enormous expense, they asked around and found that James Braid was working on Kirriemuir golf course just then. A discreet 'phone call to Kirrie and Braid was asked to call in at Edzell when he had a spare minute, to give his opinion on the new layout. There is no record that James Braid ever got the message because the Green Committee met on the course a time or two after that and planned their own alterations with no further reference to James Braid. Since the alterations have always been credited to James Braid, it is assumed that he must have approved the committee's work somewhere along the line.

Somewhere else along the line the committee deftly switched the vote from Scheme 3 to Scheme 2 by starting off on the Scheme 3 plan for the clubhouse and then, on 20 October 1924, suggesting that a footbridge was essential. When J. McIntyre proposed the motion 'That the Course be altered so as to start and finish at the Club House and for this purpose a Footbridge be erected over the Railway and that the Committee be empowered to carry out the Scheme forthwith and to decide upon all necessary details.' the committee 'unanimously agreed to support it at the half-yearly meeting.' Thus does the Committee of Edzell Golf Club serve its members, for their reversal of the club's democratic decision was by far the best plan. The original rejection of Scheme 2 by the members had been largely due to the railway company's terms for allowing a footbridge.

These terms were basically the usual railway terms for such demands but this time the railway company kept control. They remembered their 1903 embarrassment and approached this deal with rather more circumspection. They made the club build the bridge to the railway company's specification and under the railway company's supervision. They then levied a nominal annual rent. The bridge was built and proved of great benefit to all, but the club could claim no more than a fair deal at this time.

Whilst these extraneous activities were of the stuff of drama and excitement, the daily routine of club business was still being conducted with scrupulous care. As in the question of sheep. This was a continual grievance voiced by the non-farming members against the farming fraternity. The farmers couldn't see all that good grazing going to waste: the others could tolerate sheep only with mint sauce.

Even before the course was first built, grazing it had been an important consideration. In the Hon. C. M. Ramsay's discussion with the provisional committee on 18 January 1896, he had stated that 'The Club would not have the right of grazing till after Martinmas 1896.' In 1896 every man in Edzell Golf Club knew that Martinmas was the 11th of November—term day. On 4 February 1897, John Shiell, writing for C. M. Ramsay, had informed the club that they could now go ahead and let the grazing. He added that Lord Dalhousie was also 'prepared to grant a sum of Fifty Pounds to be expended in labour on the green in such a way as the Committee may approve.' That was just two more of the many gifts from the Dalhousie family to Edzell Golf Club. These regular infusions from the Earl kept the life blood flowing in Edzell Golf Club.

When the grazing came to the Club it provided a valuable addition to the funds over many years. The amount varied with the number of sheep and the length of the let, but it is reassuring to note that, from the start, the interests of the sheep were represented, appropriately, by David Lamb.

The only time that the Earl and the club seemed to be in anything less than full agreement was on that very subject—sheep. During the 1914–18 War, the club finances were at rock bottom, the Government was ordering the club to let part of the course for grazing and to plough up most of the rest whilst the club's income was rapidly diminishing. At this point they decided to suspend mechanical cutting and let the grazing of the whole course. An immediate offer of £30 from a committee member, W. C. Gowans, was accepted because the committee knew that he would balance his own interests with those of the club and look after the course.

As soon as the decision was made public, the club had a letter from 15 Hyde Park Gardens, W.1. The Earl roasted them. Why had the grazing been let 'without competition at an exceedingly low rent?'. Why had it not been advertised? Why had it not been brought up before a full, general, meeting. The letter ended: 'my great fear is that through this decision the Course may be deteriorated to the disadvantage, not only of the Members, but also of my Feuers in Edzell who depend upon the visiting golfers for a considerable part of their income.' Once again we see the importance of Edzell Golf Club to Edzell.

With a positive but placatory letter to the Earl and a skilful and protracted

Sam Edwards.

correspondence with the Ministry of Agriculture, the Club was able to weather—if one may be allowed the pun—the storm. The Earl accepted the explanation and the War ended before they had to plough up the course.

We may now return to the new clubhouse. The referendum had decided on Scheme 3 and Scheme 2 had been implemented, as shown. On Saturday, 11 July 1925, Sir Harry Hope, Member of Parliament for the County, formally opened the new building on a day of glorious sunshine and general rejoicing for the members. He made a congratulatory speech to the club, then Sam Edwards, the Captain, drove off the first ball on the redesigned course.

In Sir Harry Hope's speech, after congratulating the members on their enterprise in providing such a commodious and handsome clubhouse, he went on to say that he 'could imagine no greater happiness for those who desired reasonable recreation than to come to Edzell with its fine air, its excellent golf course, and, judging by the reception he had received that day, the kindly and hospitable members of that Club'.

That first drive by Sam Edwards must have been no more than a formality, because the company immediately retired for lunch and only after a prolonged repast, with copious toasts, did they embark on a full game. In the hallowed hush of the summer-scented eve, the results were announced:

Shcratsh: 1st C. Ferrier 78
H-Ha-Handicup: 1st C. P. Will (88–15) 73

The mellow mood that evening in the clubhouse must have unwittingly set the pattern for a thousand club competitions since. The only difference these pioneers could have known would be the pervading smell of new paint.

Edzell Golf Club was now established almost as we know it today. The new clubhouse and the new course layout with the connecting footbridge to the new second tee, set the pattern we still follow—bar the railway and the footbridge which have gone.

First reports on the new course were entirely favourable, the extra yardage of 534 yards was particularly approved and all seemed set for a spell of renewed tranquillity. It lasted about two weeks.

To understand the full implications of this next episode, one must again retrace one's steps a pace or two. Edzell's first professional was G. M. Robb—always addressed by members as 'Robb'—who had previously been with Grantown-on-Spey and Eastbourne. He was appointed to Edzell in 1906 and part of his initial agreement had been that a workshop should be built for his use. Now that the new clubhouse was there, Robb's shed was replaced by a new workshop-cum-caddies' shelter beside the gate to the Glenesk Hotel's grounds. Along from that was a shed, built by Craigie, a clubmaker from Montrose, in 1905. When Craigie had been given permission to set up shop in 1905, the same meeting had raised the wages of Robertson the Greenkeeper to 25 shillings a week and reaffirmed his 'privilege to sell clubs as formerly'.

That had set the scene for just a modicum of trouble over the next few years as to who should sell what, where, when and to whom. Robb, Craigie and Robertson were all in direct competition to sell clubs and balls to the members and now, with the appointment of a steward for the clubhouse, another claimant was going to be introduced. That particular problem rumbled on for years but the immediate concern for the club was to clear up the space behind the clubhouse where Robb's new workshop was. With the old sheds dotted around it, there were the makings of a shanty town there and the gate to the Glenesk Hotel added to the confusion by allowing folk to take a shortcut and avoid using the new entrance to their bonny new building. That was the background to the 'next business'.

It started on 22 July 1925. Miss Macdonald, of the Glenesk Hotel Company, wrote in to ask that the company take over the bridge and gate at the back of the hotel 'for making access from the lawn of the hotel to the golf course alongside Robb's workshop'.

The golf club's response was immediate: 'After discussion it was agreed that the bridge to be removed and the gate be closed and that all parties should use the main entrance to the golf course and that the bridge and gate be not given over to the Glenesk Hotel Company'.

As soon as this had been done and the hotel grounds sealed off, the Glenesk Hotel Company fired back an apparent bull's eye which seemed set to sink the Club without trace:

It has been reported to the Directors of the above Company that the footbridge across the burn at the back of the hotel leading to the Golf Course has been removed on the instructions of your Committee. The footbridge belongs to the Hotel Company, permission to erect it having been obtained from Lord Dalhousie through his factor and the Directors are very much surprised that your Committee should have taken it on themselves to remove the bridge and lock the access gate without consulting them.

The Directors regard your Committee's action as an unwarranted interference with the Company's property and we have been instructed to write you requesting your Committee to replace the footbridge forthwith and repair the gate.

There didn't seem to be much that the club could do about that, but hang on; we know Edzell Golf Club. The hotel company's letter was sent on 12 August 1925. The club's reply was sent on the 13th. Apart from all else, that illustrates the efficiency of the Forfarshire postal service in 1925. The Club's reply was succinct—one full broadside that blew the opposition out of the water:

Dear Sirs,

I am favored [sic] with your letter of 12th inst. with reference to the footbridge across the burn at the back of the Glenesk Hotel.

I have seen the Factor to the Earl of Dalhousie who informs me that he did not grant permission to the Hotel Company to erect the bridge. If his predecessor did so, you might kindly let me know the date on which this permission was given.

The footbridge and gate were erected by the Golf Club and we have vouchers to show that they were paid by the Golf Club. The Feu Charter of the Glenesk Hotel Company gives no right of access to the golf course as the boundary is the Wishop Burn.

I shall be glad to hear from you at your convenience.

Yours faithfully,
(Sgd.) Chas. Ferrier, Secretary.

There was no reply from the Glenesk Hotel Company. The next words from them didn't come until January, 1930, when a polite little note from the company asked, somewhat deferentially, if they might be permitted to put a footbridge across the burn for the convenience of hotel visitors. The club agreed, somewhat patronisingly, and immediately laid down some pretty stiff conditions including 'an annual sum of one shilling for the privilege'. There followed four pages of closely written foolscap with eight numbered paragraphs and a 'lastly' binding the hotel company into a legal obligation that would have safeguarded every fiscal requirement of the Forth Railway Bridge. Edzell Golf Club has always been well served by its professionally qualified members.

So ended the sparring match between club and hotel, and amicable relations were resumed. Hotel and club have enjoyed a mutually beneficial relationship ever since. From 1896 to 1925 the club had used the Glenesk Hotel billiards room as its clubhouse—Boxes 5 shillings per annum extra—and, bar the odd few neighbourly exchanges over the fence, everyone had been happy. The proximity of club and hotel has always been an advantage to each. It was a sad day when

On the 18th green, 1932.

members carried their things out of the billiards room for the last time.

The new clubhouse was an immediate success and a thing of beauty and joy. Conversely, its very success fomented the grumbling appendix of complaint that still affected the course. Even the patriarchal Hon. C. M. Ramsay was thinking up new criticisms. He was now able to say, with a chorus of support, 'With a clubhouse like that, why can't we have a course to match it?'

By 1930, Bob Simpson's original course had been chipped away by annual alteration and the continual modifications of successive green committees. Green committees are like that. They are prone to fantasise and have to be continually reined on the curb. In this case they had gone too far and the reins were in the hands of the members. The green committee was pulled up short and another, radical, change was ordered. It came in 1933.

James Braid and the New Design, 1933–34

If there was some doubt about James Braid's involvement in the 1925 course reconstruction, there was no doubt about his contribution to the 1933 design. With Edzell Golf Club's customary exercise of prudence, they had waited till James Braid came up to play in the Open at St Andrews before asking him to visit Edzell and advise the club on possible course alterations. In due time Braid visited the club and went round the course with the green committee, outlining his plans. His subsequent report is appended.

The committee put the report to the club and it was agreed to go ahead as advised with the exception of the last three holes. It was felt that Braid's plans for a new 16th hole and radical changes to the 17th and 18th were just a shade too drastic. There was endless discussion and much heat generated before the members would even agree to implement Braid's plan up to the 15th. They then settled for leaving the last three existing holes as they were, except that the green at the

The finish, 1932.

Watching the finish.

17th should be brought back in line with the 18th tee and that completely new tees should be made for the 17th and 18th holes. These alterations were started immediately and completed over the next couple of years.

When this lot had been done and the 17th hole moved around several times in the next few years, the course looked pretty much as we see it today. Since 1895 the biggest difference to the casual observer was in the number of trees. Originally the course was practically treeless, then successive green committees adopted a tree-planting programme, and now the fairways were being outlined with trees. This policy is still very much in operation.

The year 1934 was of some significance to the club. A new lease for the next twenty-five years was being negotiated. When the Dalhousie Estates provisionally offered a contract at £100 per annum, it was immediately and unanimously accepted by the club. The terms were so favourable that the club immediately tabled a motion thanking the Dalhousie family for their continued support and assistance. The motion 'resolved to record in the minutes their grateful thanks to the Earl of Dalhousie for his courteous and generous treatment of the club'. There is no doubt that Edzell Golf Club could not have survived long without constant support and cash from Dalhousie Estates. This minute shows that the club has always been appreciative of the fact.

Such friendly co-operation between the various 'classes' is something we find hard to accept nowadays. Even though society was rigidly stratified and strict division was maintained, it didn't mean that they were always at each other's throats. Landlord and tenant must always have a mutual interest and the old system—whilst totally unacceptable nowadays—was an accepted and practical reality. For the most part folk got on well together.

These glory days of Edzell are recalled by Mrs D. Smith Ferguson—*née* Dora Wilson—the present doyenne of Edzell Ladies (Golf and other). Dora tells of the fun she had—with all the Edzell folk—when the Maharaja of Alwar came to Invermark Lodge for the season, in the early thirties.

On the appointed day a special train pulled into Edzell Station and the Maharaja, Maharani and party descended. Lord and Lady Elphinstone, who were already installed at Invermark as hosts, welcomed them to Edzell. The whole entourage then entered a procession of cars that drew slowly out of the station and along the High Street, bound for Invermark. The entire population of the village, augmented by hundreds of visitors, lined the streets right out to the Muir to cheer the passing show. Edzell revelled in such events in those days.

Later in that same season the Maharaja was visited at Invermark by the Duke and Duchess of York with their two daughters, the Princesses Elizabeth and Margaret. Again the population of Edzell lined the streets to cheer. Mrs Ferguson remembers that occasion particularly, for on the way home that afternoon David Smith Ferguson first asked her to go to the pictures with him in Brechin that night. 'Going to the pictures' in Brechin then was the equivalent of holidaying in Spain together now—but more binding, obviously.

They knew what was on at the Brechin picture-house because it was advertised on the billboard on the side wall of Dora's father's smithy. A man used to walk—yes, walk—out from Brechin every week to put up the bills. If he was lucky, he cadged a lift back in the guard's van of the Brechin train with Willie Moir. Otherwise he walked back. It was a shock and a blow to everyone in Edzell and the Club when 'Smith' died in March, 1994.

In June, 1934, when the new lease of the course was still being worked out, the *People's Journal* carried a letter from an Edzell resident and golfer complaining of his treatment on Edzell Golf Course by Edzell Golf Club members. The complainant was a five-shilling man who felt that his rights were being usurped when club members claimed precedence over him on the course. The matter was immediately raised at a committee meeting and it was decided that no action need be taken, but the captain, F. A. Ferguson, drew up a resolution which was submitted for inclusion in the new proposed lease.

The wee man who had written to the *People's Journal* had inadvertently stuck his pen into a busy bees' byke. His letter appeared at the beginning of June. By the 15th a new Lease of Resolution, suitably phrased and amplified, was incorporated into the new lease to ensure that henceforth the club and the proprietors should have absolute and total jurisdiction over members, residenters, visitors, ladies, juniors and gangrel bodies, accompanied or unaccompanied by dogs. The actual statement in the lease runs:

Permanent Residenters and Feuars in the Drainage District of Edzell shall be entitled to play on the Course at an annual charge of Five shillings payable in advance. Players under this Rule shall have no voice in the management of the Club or Course and shall not be entitled to the use of the Club House or to claim any further privileges and shall give precedence on the Course to Members, therefore it is hereby agreed between the parties hereto that the said rule shall not be cancelled or altered without the consent of the proprietors, but always under the express declaration that the said Rule and these presents confer nothing more than a privilege or concession, voluntary on the part of the joint granters and do not and shall not create in said third parties any claim or claims as of right either in the subjects let or otherwise and shall not prevent the tenants, the said Edzell Golf Club, from exercising control over the privilege or concession thereby conferred nor debar them from taking such steps as they may deem expedient to prevent any abuse thereof; and it is hereby agreed and declared that the tenants shall make and enforce a rule prohibiting dogs from being taken on the lands hereby let.

The significance of all that is that it marks the formal erosion of the privileges granted to the Feuars of Edzell by the Rt. Hon. C. M. Ramsay—and done at a

T. Maule Guthrie.

time when the Hon. C. M. was still an active member of the club. At a cursory glance it would seem that Fred Ferguson's resolution had been intended simply to safeguard the interests of the Edzell residenters, but the converse is equally, if implicitly, valid. The consent of the proprietors could now allow the privileges of the residenters to be withdrawn, if sought by the club.

When word of the new lease was leaked to Edzell—as it was about two minutes after it was finalised—a request was submitted by a deputation of Edzell residenters for clarification of the rumours. The deputation was then invited to a meeting with Edzell Golf Club Committee and the whole question of privileges and total lack of 'rights' was explained. It resounds to the credit of the residenters that they immediately sent in a letter of thanks to the committee for the courtesy of the explanation.

In all these affairs, the interests of Edzell Golf Club were very adequately represented by the Club Captain, F. A. Ferguson. Fred Ferguson was a lawyer and Town Clerk of Brechin and as canny a negotiator as any golf club ever fielded. Fred was a captain who steered Edzell Golf Club with a steady hand. I knew him well.

Fred Ferguson.

Copy of Report of James Braid, Walton Heath

Walton Heath Golf Club,
Tadworth,
Surrey.
11th July, 1933.

The Committee,
Edzell Golf Club.

Gentlemen,

Having been invited by you to report, etc., on the Course, I visited there on the 30th ult. and have pleasure in stating that I found it in wonderful condition considering the long drought. Going carefully over each hole I herewith submit the following suggestions for your approval.

No. 1   Construct a bunker covering left third of green, 15 yrds. from Green, height of bank 2′6″.

No. 2   Fill in centre bunker.
         Construct a bunker on right, 200 yds. from tee, 14 yds. from fence, bank 3 ft.
         Construct a bunker on right, 380 yds from tee. Pot 2 ft. deep, 20 yds from fence.
         Construct a bunker on right of Green, Pot 18″ deep.
         Construct a bunker on left of Green, 8 yds. closer in.

No. 3   Construct a bunker on left, 150 yds., 12 yds. into fairway. Pot 2 ft. deep.
         Construct a bunker on right 210 yds, 5 yds. into fairway, 14 yds. long, bank 3′6″.
         Construct a bunker three pots at Green.
         Extend Green further back.

No. 4   Construct new tee farther back.
         Construct bunker on right centre, 95 yds. 10 yds long, pot 2′ deep.
         Fill in 18 yds. of bunker from right.
         Construct bunker on right, 170 yds., 12 yds. long, bank 3′6″.
         Construct a bunker on right 290 yds., 30 yds. from fence; bank 2′6″.
         Construct two bunkers at green, pots 18″ deep.

No. 5   Lower part of bunker on left.
         Construct bunker, 210 yds., 8 yds. into fairway, bank 4 ft. 14 yds long.
         Draw in bunker on left 6 yds. i.e. narrow entrance.
         Construct two bunkers at green pots.
         Extend Green nearer to edge of hill.

No. 6   Re-feature new Green as shown on plan.
         Construct diagonal cross bunker 140 yds. from Tee.

No. 7   Construct new Tee, 50 yds. back on hill.
         Lower bank of bunker approx. 18″ as advised on spot.
         Construct pot at back of Green.

No. 8 Construct bunker on left, 190 yds., 10 yds. into fairway, bank 3 ft.
Draw existing bunkers at Green closer in, even if part nearest Green is left grass only.
Construct a bunker on right far corner of Green.
Leave about 10 ft. semi-rough at back.

No. 9 Fill in right portion of bunker.

No. 10 Extend Green and bunker at sides and back.

No. 11 Construct bunker on right just short of Green. Pot.
Construct bunker on left centre of Green. Pot.

No. 12 Construct bunker 160 yds. right centre, 15 yds., bank 2′6″.
Construct bunker on left front corner of Green.

No. 13 Construct a bunker on left, 190 yds., 14 yds. into fairway, bank 3 ft.
Fill in bunker on right short of Green.
Construct bunker on right front of Green, pot 2 ft deep,
Construct bunker on left centre of Green, pot 2 ft. deep.

No. 14 Construct another Tee on right, leave all broom, etc.

No. 15 Lower bank on centre bunker for visibility.
Draw in pot bunker on left close and construct another at back.

No. 16 Advise a new hole here as I consider the last four holes the weak part of course.
Construct Tees close to wood and play dog-leg hole on to a new Green to be constructed close to present 18th tee.

No. 17 Construct new Tee close to present 17th Green and play on to Spion Kop Green.
Construct a bunker of left. Pot.

No. 18 Construct new Tee. Hole will be played slightly dog-leg.
Construct bunker left centre, 350 yds., 16 yds., bank 3 ft.

Yours faithfully
(Sgd.) Jas. Braid.

A Spell of Relative Calm

With the new clubhouse and the refurbished course, Edzell Golf Club entered one of its spells of relative calm. Relative, because a golf club can never really know absolute calm. There are always the complaints. Every golfer who completes his round reserves the right to complain about the course, the secretary, the weather and his opponent's handicap—usually in that order. Up until 1933 complaints about the course were frequently justified; now they were merely frivolous. Fred Ferguson could cope with any problems posed by that class of complainer. As the Ferguson of Ferguson and Will, Solicitors, Brechin, Fred was well trained to dismiss the importunate. The genuine complaint was heard and attended to. Now that Braid's new course was being adopted and built, one of the oldest complaints in Edzell's book started to appear again with disturbing regularity: the greens.

The greens were not good. More and more golfers were coming off the 18th muttering to themselves—and others—about the shocking state of the putting surfaces. Fred Ferguson knew they were right. He and his secretary, Sam Edwards (Factor to Dalhousie Estates), played together regularly and they knew as well as anyone the state of the greens. With typical Edzell Golf Club efficiency, they went to the top for assistance.

In March 1934, the Green Committee of Edzell Golf Club met on the course and went over the course with Mr I. G. Lewis of the Board of Greenkeeping Research, Bingley, Yorkshire, to get his advice regarding the state of the greens. It had been, as you may remember, a particularly dry summer in 1933, and this was held to be partly responsible; but the man Lewis feared more. His advice was that a detailed study of the greens should be undertaken at once to isolate the trouble and prescribe a remedy. When this had been completed, a full report was submitted to the club and was accepted.

In essence, the main points of the report were that the greens had been severely scorched by the preceding dry summer and that they suffered particularly because of the constant use of mechanical mowers. In the words of the original: 'in addition the surface on all the greens is extremely consolidated, this condition having resulted from dry weather and the continued use of the motor machine. The use of motor mowers cannot be too severely deprecated and it is strongly advised that hand machines be substituted.' There were six closely written pages in the report analysing the trouble, outlining the treatment and detailing the specific recipes:

For re-seeding
    40% New Zealand browntop
    30% Cheurings fescue
    30% True creeping red fescue
For fertilising
    2 parts Nitro-chalk
    3 parts Dried blood
    5 parts Peruvian guano
For top-dressing
    40 parts by weight soil
    30 parts by weight Lawnol
    10 parts by weight 1/16 mesh wood charcoal
    20 parts by weight sand

Detailed instructions for the application of the above, combined with spike-rolling and chain harrowing were immediately put into effect and only another dry summer postponed an effective result. At this point the committee called in Ewan Small of Small Brothers, Seedsmen, Brechin, who said that the whole trouble was caused by lack of water on the course, particularly on the greens, and advocated the installation of a piped water supply. After much discussion and the expression of powerful emotion, it was decided to go ahead with a pneumatic pressure scheme from Messrs Walker & Duncan, Aberdeen.

In the spring of 1935 a demonstration of Edzell Golf Club's new sprinkler watering system for the greens was held to general acclaim. For the technically minded, it included a 5 h.p. Petter diesel engine with water-cooling apparatus, silencer, etc., coupled to a treble ram pump, steel pneumatic tank, complete with 3-inch diameter suction pipe, valves, gauges, meter and all fittings. The engine and pump were capable of delivering 2,100 gallons per hour against a total head of 200 feet and with a pressure of not less than 60 to 70 feet at the highest green when delivering 7 gallons per minute at this green. The water was led to 18 hydrants—one per green—each connected to the terminal end of an asbestos cement branch and each equipped with a cast-iron ground box with hinged lid. For attachment to the hydrants there were five 'Majestic' revolving sprinklers and five lengths of one-inch hose pipe, 60 feet long.

Between them the greenkeeping research wallahs, Walker & Duncan and Ewan Small, combined with a drop of rain at just the right time did wonders for the Edzell greens.

As the years passed, the founder-members of the club were dropping off one by one, but there was always a hard core of old boys keeping an eye on the young upstarts. There is never a time in a golf club when the old boys are not required to counter the iconoclasm of the upstart young. The ethos of Edzell Golf Club was moulded and nurtured by this group of patriarchs whose influence still obtains. If the visitor to Edzell Golf Club today senses an ambient air of welcome and friendship within its portals, it is the direct result of the standards maintained by the old boys he sees around him.

In 1934 the Rev. T. C. Sturrock was made a life member. In April 1936 the Hon. C. M. Ramsay died. The 1930s saw the demise of the Edzell old guard, but the 1930s also saw Edzell Golf Club reach a peak of popularity and success as a direct result of their foresight and industry—and this when the 1930s were years of international turmoil. Wars raged in Spain, Africa and Europe. Hitler steadily strengthened his grip on Germany and the Continent. British governments lurched, as is the way of British governments, from crisis to crisis, and Edzell Golf Club basked in spring promise, summer sunshine and autumn gold. Little wonder that, as the tensions of political life increased, so the joys of golf on Edzell Golf Course also increased.

There is a special joy in Edzell golf course. To stand on the first tee and savour the *frisson* of anticipation is a rare privilege. To play the course and surmount its varied intricacies is a sustained pleasure, but to play Edzell in high summer, in basking sunshine, in a mixed foursome, is bliss. Larks trill high in the caller air o'er Edzell: red squirrels frolic freely on its fairways: cock pheasants, so tame that they forbear to fly, step languidly from the path whilst yellow hammers, like loosed canary birds, pick unconcernedly the green. There is a wealth of wildlife on Edzell Golf Course and yet it holds coigns of tranquillity and calm. The river bank that bounds the 8th green and the 9th tee contains a miniature Eden. The eminence of the 16th green commands a panorama of hill and vale and river line that delights the soul. Over all the Caterthuns keep guard, and who knows that the Iron Age is not so-called simply because they had not then developed the long woods?

Into the 1930s, Edzell golf club was still using horses for course maintenance.

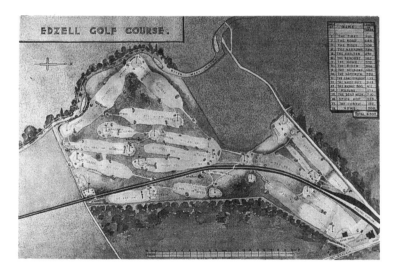

Plan of the course, 1935.

At 35 shillings a week—and orra baists at 7 shillings a day—Mains of Edzell hired out the power units to work the course. Motor mowers were coming in, as the greenkeeping research boys were quick to deplore, and the 1930s saw the end of regular horse power on the course. Until then the horse set the pace; in those halcyon days, and golfers were the happier for it.

The War Years

As 1939 approached the calm of Edzell was disturbed by the arrival of the Services. Edzell RAF Station, the Royal Naval establishment at HMS *Condor*, Arbroath, and the Flying School at Montrose were the main stations, but several other flying fields existed on farm lands around the county. Edzell Golf Club was much patronised. As in the Boer War and the Great War, the club extended privilege to members absent on service and the servicemen stationed in the area.

In March 1941, Gilbert M. Robb, the professional, died. He had been professional at Edzell since 1907 and had seen the club through its early years of growth. A letter of condolence was sent to his wife and son, including an excerpt from the club minutes which said that he had been professional for over 34 years and during that long time had been a faithful and honest servant and had carried out his duties to the satisfaction of the committee and the members of the club. The committee expressed their deep sympathy with his wife and son in their bereavement.

Gilbert Robb was succeeded by F. M. Dean, of Wyke Green Golf Club, who was appointed on a temporary basis and a provisional contract on 1 May 1941, subsequently reviewed and made permanent on 3 September 1943.

In November 1941, Lieut. J. M. Forster, of HMS *Condor*, wrote to the club thanking the members for allowing naval personnel to use the course and offering to pay an *en bloc* membership subscription to cover all Condor golfers. The club replied with thanks to the lieutenant but declined to accept payment. The Royal Navy must enjoy the same privileges as the other Services. In reply to that letter, Lieut. Forster sent the club a framed aerial photograph of Edzell Golf Course, taken by one of the HMS *Condor* planes. This photograph now hangs in the men's bar of the clubhouse.

All during the war—and even after—there were repeated skirmishes with the Agricultural Committee for Angus who wanted bits of the course ploughed up and other bits let out for grazing. A sub-committee of Messrs Edwards, Will and Ferrier was appointed to handle that lot, and after prolonged negotiations, the Agricultural Executive Committee issued their Order No. 84528 and, in 1942, eight acres of Edzell Golf Course were put to the plough. The most the sub-committee could do was to limit the area and ensure that the let went to James Raitt, Smiddyhill, a member, and that the grazing was also safely let to golfers.

In October 1944, Dean, the professional, resigned and the club decided to carry

44

on without a full-time professional until things improved. It wasn't until 1946 that a replacement was appointed, and R. Dornan, the professional at Forfar Golf Club, was signed on.

Bob Dornan had been professional at Forfar since 1931, and in 1932 he won the Scottish Professional Championship over the Forfar course. In 1933 he became professional at South Staffs. Golf Club, Wolverhampton, but rejoined Forfar in 1944 and was promoted to Edzell on 1 April 1946. He resigned from Edzell in 1948 and was replaced by E. D. Bisset from Stonehaven Golf Club.

The Post-War Recovery

In this immediate post-war period the club was going through a recovery phase as a result of neglect during the war years with under-staffing and course cropping, and the immediate need was for funds to start the process of regeneration. Every golf club was experiencing the same difficulties at this time and Edzell just buckled to it with typical application. To add to their problems, the steward, Mrs Gordon, resigned and was replaced by Mrs Gibson from Dalhousie Golf Club, Carnoustie; then in May, 1947, Sam Edwards died. For many years Sam Edwards had been a stalwart of the club as member, committee member, and captain for several years. His loss was a sore blow to the club, for Mr Edwards was one of those men who had worked tirelessly in the interests of the club since

A group of well-known Dundee business men who played at Edzell in 1948 for the cup specially donated by George Thomson, Flax Manufacturer. *Back row, left to right*: T. Wilson, HM Inspector of Taxes; A. J. Strachan, Managing Director Wm. Hunter & Co., Wellgate; A. Mathewson, Tea Merchant; George McLeod, Jute Merchant, Calcutta; George Thomson, James David, Merchant. *Front row, left to right*: A. L. Proctor, Chartered Surveyor; A. ('Sandy') McGill.

the day he joined. That day was 6 June 1914, and for 33 years he had served the Club faithfully.

T. W. Wood, the Captain, instigated a number of fund-raising measures, and his successor, C. Gordon Mackie, carried them on, but the perennial cry of one group of members, to raise the subscription, was always countered and nullified by the majority. It wasn't until April, 1949—under N. J. H. Goodchild as Captain—that the annual subscription was raised from two guineas to three guineas. Heads were shaken in Edzell when that figure was first quoted, but it was explained by the committee that three guineas was reckoned to be as high as the subscription would ever be required to go. The hope was expressed that in a year or two it might be reduced again. Subsequent events have tended to disprove that particular delusion.

One of the fund-raising ideas and publicity functions that was started was the Edzell Golf Club's annual open amateur championship. This was a portentous move for the club. At the Edzell open tournament on 11 June 1949, the winner broke the course record with a second round of 69. With his first round of 78 he finished four strokes ahead of the runner-up and completed what turned out to be a memorable day for Edzell Golf Club. That record-breaking Edzell Open Champion of 1949 was none other than J. B. Webster. Jim Webster, who subsequently became Edzell's own professional—one of the best golfers and club professionals that any golf club could ever have. Jim played, taught, supported and encouraged generations of Edzell golfers, and not one ever had a word to say against him. Jim Webster came from a family of golfers and, happily, the dynasty has provided Edzell with its present professional, Jim's son, Alastair, another in the same line of succession:

Jim's winning card read: Out – 354443534 – 35
$$\begin{array}{r} \text{In} \; - 444434335 - \underline{34} \\ \underline{69} \end{array}$$

In September of that year, 1949, a new professional record for the course was set by the club professional, E. D. Bisset, with a card one stroke behind Jim Webster's:

E. D. Bisset's card read Out: 443343544 – 34
$$\begin{array}{r} \text{In:} \quad 454434435 - \underline{36} \\ \underline{70} \end{array}$$

The Open Championship had been instrumental in bringing Edzell's name once more into public prominence, and, for a time, things looked better. Fund–raising schemes were organised, and with a concerted drive to attract new members it seemed that things might be improving all round, but always there is one concerned member for whom things do not improve quickly enough.

In this instance that member wrote a letter to the Secretary, William Wyse, in

Looking back from behind the 1st green to the clubhouse and the new shop.

which he lambasted Edzell Golf Club for everything from the state of the towels in the men's room, the failure to provide a cup of tea when requested and the treatment of visitors in the clubhouse to the state of the course generally, the shrinkage of the greens specifically, the failure to cut the fairways properly and the total inefficiency of the club staff in every particular. His immediate suggestion—couched in the most temperate language and explicit logic—was to sack the entire crew with the possible exception of one assistant greenkeeper (name unfortunately not given) and start again from scratch. His peroration was:

> Edzell Golf Club must be put into such a condition that we can again have the activity which was evident before the War and in my opinion until the course is put into such a condition we are bound to be faced with a drop in revenue from the visitors and parties who contribute so much to the club. I feel that with the loss of revenue following upon the loss of the Panmure Arms Hotel, the club must look farther afield and attract visitors to come to the course. The course should also be available to visitors for Sunday golf and the present restrictions removed.
>
> These suggestions are submitted in a spirit to contribute something to assist in meeting the situation which is now facing us and are not made in any way as a criticism of the present Committee of Management. I trust they will be accepted in this spirit and that they will assist in some measure to help to formulate a policy which will result in a revival of interest in the affairs of Edzell Golf Club, of which we are all rightly proud, and which I feel only requires stimulation to achieve something worthwhile in the future.

The reference to the Panmure Arms was made because it had just been burned

The 17th green and Dalhousie Lodge.

down and the club feared that the many Panmure Arms residents and visitors would be lost to the golf course. Fortunately no-one was lost in the fire.

That letter was a gem of its kind. Into a most acceptable draught the writer had introduced the distilled essence of 'Disgusted', Tunbridge Wells, 'Concerned Member', Edzell, and even a drop from old 'Pro Bono Publico' himself. The Committee received it. The Committee read it and by the twin camps of Caterthun, the Committee acted on it. That letter set in train a scourging and a purging that stripped Edzell Golf Club to its very bones. Every man jack on the committee set to and reviewed his remit. Standards were restored, duties fulfilled and obligations observed. Edzell Golf Club reassumed its pristine state.

Over the next few months and years every aspect of the club was overhauled and improved. In 1953 they cleared £700 from a prize draw and as much again from other projects. In 1954, E. D. Bisset was replaced by David Dunlop from Torwoodlea Golf Club, Galashiels, and the whole organisation and arrangement of staff duties were reviewed. The course improved, the clubhouse improved, the attitude of members and staff alike improved. The annual subscription, despite the reassurances of 1949, was banged up to five guineas and a joining fee of three guineas proposed. This was a most traumatic time for Edzell Golf Club but it was also the most energetic and effective time in its history and it stemmed directly from that letter on 14 April 1952. The name of A. Drummond, Esq., Letter Writer, should be limned in gold above the portals of Edzell Golf Club today.

A lady on the 7th tee.

Alec Drummond was a manager of the Union Bank in Brechin, a stalwart of Brechin Amateur Dramatic Society and an adjudicator at national festivals. Obviously a man well qualified to put an ailing golf club back on its feet. His letter provided just the stimulus required.

So effective were the measures adopted that by October 1955 the Committee passed a special vote of commendation and thanks to Ewan Small, the green convener, and Dave Jolly and his staff, the greenkeepers. They were proud of the course once again.

The Diamond Jubilee, 1956

When Edzell Golf Club Jubilee had been marked in 1946, the immediate post-war problems of rationing, restricted supplies, austerity and the like had precluded any celebration of the event. Now, in 1956, it was decided to hold a Diamond Jubilee dinner-dance in celebration. The details and arrangements were delegated to Mr. W. F. Howe, and that ensured the success of the whole affair from the outset. Mr. W. F. Howe was a man of some ability.

In his address to the company at the dinner, the Chairman, Captain R. G.

Captain R. G. Duke RN.

Duke, R.N. (Retd.) and now Captain of Edzell Golf Club, gave a brief history of the club and read a telegram from the Rev. T. C. Sturrock. The Rev. Sturrock, one of the co-founders of the Club, was now over 90 years of age and living in Edinburgh. He and Mr 'Willie' Johnston of Brechin were the only two of the original 56 founder members still 'going strong'.

Captain Duke outlined the story of the club and included a reminiscence of his playing golf on the original six holes on the Muir in the summer of 1895. His memory of that game was vivid because he had been playing behind 'an old gentleman in a red coat' and had unfortunately hit him on the back of the neck with his ball. That had caused what the Captain recalled as a 'considerable stooshie'. He could not claim that as a reason for the founding of the new club but cited it at least as a contributory factor.

The Captain's speech ended with the hope that the Club would continue to flourish and the words:

> Think of all the enjoyment these acres have given; think of all the thousands—and I mean thousands—of people who have had sport and recreation all the year round and long happy summer days of holiday golf during these sixty years, and then just think what a debt of gratitude we all owe to these few fellows who founded our Club. Surely we can say of them 'They builded better than they knew' and so, I should hope, say all of us . . .

The 7th green.

As a concomitant of all the fund and subscription raising that was going on at the time, a motion was quietly slipped in to the effect that 'The Resident's fee for those over 18 years of age be increased to £1 per year and that the rules governing their play remain as at present.'

This was proposed by Mr J. P. Gellatly and seconded by Mr A. K. Murray. Significantly, Joe and A. K. were both Brechin men. Joe Gellatly, of Gellatly's bread, and A. K. Murray, the bank manager. Their proposal signalled the end of the five-shilling sub. and it was carried unanimously. That was also the end of the Hon. C. M. Ramsay's original concession and witness to the fact that Fred Ferguson's Resolution of June 1934 was now operative. There was no question of preferential treatment on the waiting list in 1956. There was no waiting list.

Gannochy Golf Club

A word of explanation might be in order here. Back in 1902 a club for those Edzell golfers who availed themselves of the five-shilling concession tickets was founded: the Gannochy Golf Club. It represented the interests of such residents and was a properly constituted club, with members, officials, trophies, inter-club matches and social functions. It did not have a course, a clubhouse, a green staff, a professional nor any connection with or rights in, Edzell Golf Club. It had a limited use of the course and the five-shilling men had the obligation to 'give way' to Edzell Golf Club members when required.

It is not surprising that, over the years, questions of mutual concern have arisen. Generally the relationship between the two clubs has been amicable but there are records of near animosity on occasion. On such subjects as requests for 'the privilege of the green' for Gannochy competitions; the obligation to 'give precedence on the course to members'; the request to have a Gannochy noticeboard in the clubhouse (refused) and a hint of a possible difference of opinion between individuals at the Gannochy Annual Dance in the Central Hotel on 30 October 1964. Fortunately such minutiae have caused only minor blips on the computer screen of friendly relations between the two clubs, but they do require recognition. Friendly co-operation between the two has never been better than it is today.

The Subscription Debate

When the five-shilling fee was raised in 1956 to £1, there was an influx of Edzell residents into full membership. Fourteen Edzell residents joined on 16 April 1956. One of these was Mr D. S. Ferguson—'Smith' Ferguson—whose name had already featured in the club's records as a residenter. Smith Ferguson was the son of D. Ferguson, a member of the original Edzell Club on the Muir, and father of D. W. Ferguson, a present stalwart of Edzell Golf Club. In April 1959, the A.G.M. of Edzell Golf Club decreed that 'the clause whereby permanent residents and feuars in the drainage district of Edzell were entitled to play on the course at a considerably reduced charge would be withdrawn'. And that was that.

All these measures were being taken to improve the club's finances, but in 1960, when another proposal was made to increase the annual subscription, it was

'Willie' Howe

defeated because the new Secretary, W. F. Howe, had instigated a number of fund-raising schemes which were beginning to show results. W. F. Howe was one of these men whose names must be accorded special mention in any record of Edzell Golf Club.

'Willie' Howe was an ex-India wallah whose education, personality, attitude and career had made him a formidable contender in the prize ring of life. Small, square, immaculate in appearance and not given to wasting too much time in laughter, Willie Howe was a grafter. His handling of a committee was exemplary; his handling of an individual was peremptory. There are men in Edzell today who are the better for having been ticked off by Willie Howe. To hear Willie conduct one of his *Pro re nata* meetings was a lesson in judicious committee manipulation. To hear Willie rush from the clubhouse and assail some miscreant on the first tee was a lesson in applied character assassination. Willie went for you like a West Highland terrier at a rat.

The club captain at this time was Major T. P. Douglas-Murray. He and W. F. Howe made a formidable team. Major Murray was described by a contemporary as 'looking like the archetypal "wicked squire" in a Victorian melodrama'. That was possibly so but his nature belied his appearance. Despite the apparently irascible demeanour, Major Murray was a very pleasant man to know and a gentleman to work with. He was factor to Dalhousie Estates and served the interests of both Dalhousie and the golf club to the greater benefit of both.

Major T. P. Douglas-Murray.

Over the years there have been many recurring themes that have continued to exercise the Edzell committee—as they must every golf club committee. Primarily there is the subscription. There are always those members whose answer to every call for increased revenue is quite simply, 'raise the sub'. There are also those other members whose cherished ambition is, quite simply, 'don't raise the sub'. It is to Edzell Golf Club Committee's credit that they have always succeeded in maintaining an acceptable equipoise.

As an adjunct to the subscription debate there is the allied question of visiting parties. That fine balance which requires to be struck between desirable revenue and less desirable intrusion, is one which taxes the ingenuity of committees generally, and treasurers in particular. In this context Edzell Golf Club has always been especially fortunate in being able to recruit retired bankers as treasurers. Statistically, the incidence of poverty amongst retired bank managers is negligible, and they are known to conduct their clubs' accounts similarly. Whenever Edzell Golf Club has required financial sustenance, a friendly retired bank manager has always assumed responsibility for restoring solvency. One more example of the club's good husbandry!

Other recurring problems, peculiar to Edzell, have been the question of making a double green for the 4th and 11th holes and the running battle about whether to leave the 17th tee down by the railway or hoick it up the hill by the 16th green. These protracted debates have generated a fair head of steam in Edzell

The 8th (medal) tee.

over the years—as have the annual arguments about tees, fairways, bunkers, greens and who should get the buggy.

In 1958 a reorganisation of the club's staff duties saw David Dunlop restricted to serving as professional and running the shop. He was relieved of all clubhouse supervision and other responsibilities and a new steward and stewardess, John and Mrs Schierloh, Coronation Hotel, Alvaston, Derby, were appointed. Soon after that a long-serving greenkeeper, Alec Smith, retired after 39 years of 'long, good and faithful service to the club' (Captain's tribute). In March 1959 the Hon. Secretary, W. Wyse, and the Hon. Treasurer, W. Jardine, both resigned. They had served the club well for ten and five years respectively, and each was pressed to continue in office and then 'sincerely thanked for all they had done for the club during their period of office'. They were replaced by Mr Edwin Fleming as Hon. Treasurer and Mr W. F. Howe as Hon. Secretary. The name of W. F. Howe was cropping up regularly as one who was taking a very active part in club affairs.

The annual dinner dance of the club took place in the Glenesk Hotel on Friday, 1 April 1960, and the membership was now rising and stood at 211. A motion to raise the subscription from five guineas to seven guineas was withdrawn because several fund-raising projects instituted by Mr W. F. Howe were beginning to show results. The fact that 1959 had been a particularly good summer had also helped boost the club's finances and Edwin Fleming's report for 1959–60 read:

A spring morning on the 8th green.

Speaking on an estimate of the Club's income for the year to 28 February, 1960, the Honorary Treasurer reported the estimated subscriptions to be £1,035 as against £895 for the previous year. Green fees £1,390 as against £1,004 and profit off bar £1,172 as against £608. Continuing, the Honorary Treasurer reported that ignoring donations from members which may be regarded as a non-recurring item, income will show an estimated increase of £1,100. On the expenditure side, repairs and improvements to be carried out, or in the process of being carried out, amount to approximately £266. (Lockers for ladies' room £29, wiring for new cooker and new lights in dining room £37, alterations to dining room £200). This expenditure could properly be regarded as capital expenditure but in the meantime has been written off.

In view of the position shown by the estimates, it may be wise to reconsider the decision to increase the subscription by two guineas per annum with effect from 1/3/60. While the majority of members may have accepted the necessity of an increase in subscription in the light of the results for 1958–59, they may well question the justification for an increase after a year in which the Club's income has gone up by £1,100.

The new team of Major Douglas-Murray, Ed. Fleming and W. F. Howe with the new steward, John Schierloh, now set to work to put Edzell at the top of the golf club tree, and it did not take them long. With the finances secured by the judicious direction of Ed. Fleming, it was soon evident that a new spirit was motivating the whole club. Major Murray set the standards; Willie Howe implemented them. The members did what they were told to do, happily. There is no better government than a benign dictatorship.

Staff Changes

The head greenkeeper, David Jolly, retired then after over 40 years' continuous service to the club and the manner of his replacement is a measure of the way W. F. Howe worked in the interests of Edzell Golf Club. When it was first announced that Dave Jolly was to retire, Willie went straight to work. He discussed the matter with Ewan Small, the green convener, and then the two of them made a tour of all the neighbouring golf clubs. They simply looked at how the various courses were tended. They spoke casually to members about the greenkeepers' efficiency; they innocently discussed the weather and the price of grass seed with the individual greenkeepers. Soon they had decided that W. A. F. Thomson of Stonehaven Golf Club was the man they wanted.

Only then was it disclosed to W. A. F. Thomson in a most informal and incidental manner that there might, there just might, be an opening soon in Edzell Golf Club for such a man as he. He expressed interest and was thereupon invited

Looking back along the 9th.

down—for a purely speculative visit, of course—to see the Edzell course for himself. At the next committee meeting the name of W. A. F. Thomson was mentioned. It was not presented as a *fait accompli*, it was just mentioned as the kind of man that Edzell would be lucky to get. The Committee agreed with W. F. Howe and Ewan Small and the new greenkeeper was appointed. The episode was recorded on 6 September 1960, as:

> The committee proceeded to interview an applicant for the post, Mr. W. A. F. Thomson. Messrs. E. C. Small and W. F. Howe reported that they had already interviewed the applicant at his present post, Stonehaven Golf Club, and also that they had shown the applicant over Edzell golf course and all the equipment owned by the Club. The applicant stated he was quite convinced he could carry out the duties of Head Green-keeper to the satisfaction of the Committee with the assistance of one full-time Greenkeeper and perhaps one casual employee for a few weeks during the summer months. The applicant stated he was desirous of leaving his present post as he found he could not do justice to the post of Head Greenkeeper and Steward and that his wife as caretaker was not able to carry out her duties owing to a recent addition to the family, making a family of three in all. It was pointed out to the applicant that for the present no house was available in Edzell but the Club was prepared to house him in a house within the precincts of Brechin Laundry, Brechin. The applicant stated that both he and his wife had been shown over the house and that he was prepared to reside there meantime. It was stressed that every endeavour would be made to procure a house in Edzell as quickly as possible but without stating a time limit.

Across the 10th to the hills.

The post of Head Greenkeeper was then offered to the applicant at a wage of £10 per week with rent-free accommodation plus travelling allowance to Edzell during the time he resides in Brechin. The offer was accepted and it was agreed that duties would be taken over within a few days of the 10th October, 1960.

It is of interest to note here that the present-day practice of 'head-hunting' successful top business executives is no more than the original Willie Howe system for appointing head greenkeepers.

The next few years saw more changes in personnel. The professional, Dave Dunlop, was appointed to Ranfurly Castle and was replaced by Ken Storrier. E. C. Fleming was transferred from the district and replaced by Mr James Milne. At the end of 1962 the new professional was congratulated by the captain for winning the mixed foursomes at Scotscraig in partnership with Mrs David Ferguson. Mrs Ferguson started her career with Edzell Golf Club as a caddy at sixpence per round in the 1920s and she still plays a few holes regularly. Mrs Ferguson can tell you about Edzell Golf Club.

At the end of W. A. F. Thomson's first year the captain gave him a special commendation for the way he had improved the condition of the course and the general condition of the clubhouse area. Unfortunately, W. A. F. Thomson resigned in 1962 to go to Nairn Golf Club as head greenkeeper. Edzell appointed Robert Paterson as replacement. Ken Storrier then left, peremptorily, in 1963 and his replacement was R. D. W. Kerr, son of George Kerr. Robert Kerr died, only one year later, in 1964.

At the half-yearly meeting on 30 October 1963, the captain, Major T. P. Douglas Murray remarked, *inter alia*, that members present could observe that a fruit machine had been installed. All members of the committee were opposed to it in principle but all agreed it was a necessity financially. The machine was on trial and would be purchased outright in March 1964. That was indeed a black day for Edzell Golf Club—when fiscal expediency overcame moral scruple—but no more than a measure of our times.

This same meeting heard a plea from life member H. G. H. Cowell. It is reported that 'he was most adamant that members should not interdigitate'. On a cursory reading that might appear to be a criticism of the Harry Vardon grip, but a closer examination reveals it to be no more than an objection to members alternating on the tee with visiting parties. A relief for exponents of the Vardon overlap. Only Edzell Golf Club uses words like that.

When the club came to appoint a successor to Robert Kerr, there was a unanimous decision to approach one of their own members—Jim Webster. Jim Webster was an engineer working with the firm of Matrix in Brechin, Edzell Club Champion, and a member of a well-known local golfing family. Jim was persuaded to make the change, and so began one of the most harmonious relationships in the club's history. Jim Webster served Edzell Golf Club faithfully and well and made a friend of every golfer he ever dealt with. It was a severe blow

The 13th green.

to Edzell when Jim died in 1993 and the hundreds of people who packed Edzell Kirk at his funeral were testimony to that fact. Fortunately for the club, Jim Webster was succeeded by his son Alastair as professional. Alastair is one of Scotland's leading professional golfers, head of the Scottish Professional Golfers' Association and highly ranked as a tournament player. He has already publicised Edzell Golf Club worldwide.

Over the years, ever since 1903, the question of railway bridges and level crossings had plagued the club. In 1964 the matter was resolved. The Edzell-Brechin line finally closed. The metal bridge at the station was removed and the rails lifted. Thus came to an end one of the great local railway links that meant so much to the economic prosperity and social well-being of rural communities. For thirty-five years the little Brechin-Edzell trains had chugged along by Trinity, Brathinch, Inchbare and over the West Water to Edzell Golf Course and the station. The only station *en route* was Inchbare—renamed Stracathro in 1912— and the railway was one of the features of Edzell Golf Course. If you hook your drive at the fourth or the fifteenth it still is.

Passenger services had been withdrawn in 1931 when the guard, Willie Moir, flagged the last train off from Edzell with a black flag. Willie had flagged the first train off in 1896—using the regulation green flag—and served as guard for the whole span of the passenger service. Goods trains continued to use the line after 1931, but 1964 saw the end of the whole enterprise and the removal of the lines.

The short 14th.

This was a period when there had been mutterings of discontent about the state of the clubhouse, and Major Douglas-Murray had been listening. The committee voted for a refurbishment, and T. P. Douglas-Murray made it his personal responsibility to oversee a complete programme of alteration and redecoration. He worked tirelessly with the committee to ensure that the job was done as expeditiously, efficiently and acceptably as possible. When the clubhouse had been completely remodelled internally and redecorated overall, it was a paragon of its kind and it bore the stamp of Major Douglas-Murray. Only then did Major T. P. Douglas-Murray feel entitled to resign, having been captain for nine arduous years.

In his vote of thanks to Major T. P. Douglas-Murray at the A.G.M. of April 1965, Mr E. C. Small said that Major Murray had taken over the captaincy when the finances were not good and when many things had to be done. Under his wise guidance Major Murray had greatly improved the finances, and in addition the amenities of the clubhouse, with the result that today the Club was in very good shape. He asked the meeting to give a very hearty vote of thanks.

The contract for all the work in the clubhouse had been undertaken by Messrs. Ritchie and Dick of Brechin. When the job had been completed and all the accounts settled, Mr H. Dick—a club member—'was most cordially thanked for all the work done in connection with the alterations. It was particularly pleasing to note that the final accounts against the contract were actually less than the original tenders.' So pleased was the club with its new clubhouse that a joint advertisement with the Glenesk Hotel showing a composite photograph of the Hotel and Clubhouse was published—cost to the Club £5!

The ladies' section of Edzell Golf Club has always been a most amenable section. Operating as an independent unit under the aegis of the club committee, the ladies' club has existed in almost total harmony with the parent club over the years. Only occasionally have muted murmurs of complaint been heard and very seldom has any real difference of opinion been recorded. One such rare occasion occurred in September 1965 when a letter from the ladies' section requested a re-siting of the ladies' tee at the fourteenth. The matter had been raised before but nothing had been done. This time, the ladies backed their case with statistics. 'Out of 330 cards returned so far, only 41 show 3s at the 14th.' Tee re-sited forthwith and friendly relations resumed.

In the following spring a big tree planting programme was started with the green convener, Robert Inglis, working closely with the Forestry Commission in a combined effort. Once again this was a case of Edzell Golf Club putting the right man in the right place at the right time. A great part of the scenic beauty of the course today is the direct result of Bob's work. In close co-operation with Mr J. Chrystall of the Forestry Commission he arranged for the planting of trees on two acres between the 7th and 9th fairways, approximately one acre between the 5th and 7th fairways and approximately one acre between the 13th fairway and the railway. The involvement of the Forestry Commission was essential. Grants.

In addition to his tree-planting initiative, Robert Inglis conducted a general sprucing up of the course, extending the tees on ten of the holes, filling in three superfluous bunkers—as though all bunkers were not superfluous—and improving the whole set-up. By 6 April 1966 he was able to report to the committee that 14.3 acres in all had been planted with Norwegian spruce and Scots fir trees—25,000 in total. At the A.G.M. of that year the Captain, Mr J. A. Ogg, expressed sincere thanks to Mr Inglis for all the thought and work that he had put into the project. In addition, he informed the meeting that the total outlay would amount to £570 and the grant from the Forestry Commission would be £320, leaving the cost to the club at £250. 'These plantations are a growing asset and in five years' time there could be a small return and quite a handsome return in later years.' He sounded a note of warning that the asset could be dissipated if the members themselves did not look after the plantations.

It is worth bearing in mind that it is the expertise and dedication of men like Bob Inglis that has given us the splendid facilities for golf that we enjoy on Edzell Golf Course today.

Purchase of the Course: Proposals, Discussions, Improvements

One recurring topic that had exercised the minds of Edzell golfers since the inception of the club was raised formally in 1971: the purchase of the course. In July 1971 the Captain, A. J. Hunter, discussed the matter informally with Major T. P. Douglas-Murray. He wanted to know the best way of broaching the subject with Dalhousie Estates. 'Edzell Golf Club Committee was', he said, 'most anxious to approach the trustees to discuss the question of purchasing the land.' A formal application was then lodged and on 12 August a formal reply was returned:

> We act for the proprietors of Edzell Golf Course and Lord Dalhousie's Factor, Mr Durant, has passed to us your letter to him of 21st July in which you raise the question of the proposed purchase of the Golf Course by the Edzell Golf Club.
> We have been instructed to inform you that our clients are not to sell the golf course.

That, for the time being, was that. . . .

Purchasing the golf course then became just one more *cause célèbre* to add to the list of such causes—as in the perennial case of visiting parties. The visiting party problem arose through the necessity for their revenue as opposed to the nuisance of their presence. The debate still continues. In 1969 relief was expressed when the number of visiting parties—and the number in visiting parties—was drastically reduced. The record had been set in 1968 when a party of 90 turned up from the North of Scotland Hydro Board. Another party was guilty of the sin of 'introducing music to the men's lounge'. I can just imagine Willie Howe's reaction to that atrocity. Visitors to Edzell Golf Club were expected to conform to Edzell Golf Club's standards and it was Willie who was largely responsible for setting those standards. *Grâce à* Willie Howe, there is still no music in any part of Edzell Golf Club.

The next few years saw the club continue calmly on its way and few clubs are blessed with calmer ways than Edzell. In recognition of his nine years as captain and his personal responsibility for the completion of the scheme of alteration and addition to the clubhouse, Major T. P. Douglas-Murray was made a life member. The same meeting heard a proposal to increase the fee of the auditor, Mr F. D. Booth—Fred Booth—he of the totally original Freddie Booth golf stance, grip and swing—then replied that he considered his remuneration ample for the work

An aerial photograph of the course, in 1942, presented by HMS *Condor.*

done and the matter was closed. How many auditors have been known to do that?

In 1969 the annual subscription was raised. Rising costs, increased green staff, the loss of income from the reduction in the numbers of visiting parties, all contributed to the need for an increased subscription. The ordinary members' class A, over twenty-one, fee of eight guineas was bumped right up to ten guineas, a prodigious rise. Other fees were altered accordingly. With a membership now at 293, the extra money was welcomed by the committee. By the end of the year the captain, E. C. Small, was able to announce that the membership had passed the 300 mark. During the summer seven new members had joined and the number was now 308.

Despite the increase in the numbers of people wanting to play golf, the significance of Edzell as a holiday resort had waned since the end of the war. The introduction of the package holiday and the competition of Spain's 'costa cheapo' proved to be more than the bracing air of Edzell could counter. Discriminating people still holiday in Edzell, and play the golf course, but the days when pipe bands met the excursion trains and hundreds marched up the High Street to picnic on the Muir, are long gone.

The 15th — Deil's Neuk — I'll say!

Like all golf clubs, Edzell has always benefited from the support of its visitors, and one of its annual high days used to be the club v. visitors' challenge match. No competition was ever more keenly contested than the visitors' match for the A. B. Scott Cup. In 1969 the visitors' match fizzled out and the A. B. Scott Cup was re-allocated for competition by the club seniors. A knell for the death of Edzell as a holiday resort.

When the treasurer, James Milne, retired after nine years' service he was replaced by Alec (Sandy) Low. James Milne was made a life member in recognition of his sterling service to the club as treasurer and financial adviser to the committee. Bob Inglis retired at the same time from his position as green convener, and he was replaced by Robert Hall. This latter appointment was of particular significance to the club. Bob Hall, like Willie Howe, was an ex-India wallah and with two such high caste sons of the Raj in positions of authority, the club soon began to show it. For a start, the steward was given a clothing allowance to ensure his being properly and appropriately dressed when on duty, and the green staff was augmented and disciplined to ensure a continuation of the good work done by Bob Inglis.

The question of improving the clubhouse was always being raised and it became so insistent that a special general meeting was called to discuss suggestions. The meeting dismissed the whole idea out of hand with a vote For: 6 and Against: 61. The committee then adopted the alternative suggestion of providing a new professional's shop. An *ad hoc* committee of Ewan Small (captain), Willie Howe and Bob Hall was appointed. By 1971 they had a new pro's shop built on the site of the old shed. An approach was made to Messrs. Hawtree, course architects, Croydon, to have a survey done on the course with a view of having any necessary alterations done. Their report was entirely favourable to the course and only relatively minor alterations were recommended. These consisted of re-designing some bunkers and planting strategically placed trees. All the work was accepted and mainly completed by 1974.

Dr T. C. K. Marr succeeded A. J. Hunter as Captain in 1973 and the A.G.M. of that year raised the Class A subscription to £15 and proposed an entrance fee of £20. The entrance fee was held over; the subscripton was raised.

Soon after his appointment, Dr Marr stated that he was unhappy with certain aspects of the club's relationship with the Gannochy Golf Club which appeared to be divisive and not in the best interests of Edzell Golf Club. He convened a meeting between an *ad hoc* committee of the golf club and members of the Gannochy Golf Club to discuss matters. Essentially, Dr Marr wanted the Gannochy Golf Club to confine its membership to the original concept of that club, i.e. 'Residenters and feuars of the village of Edzell'. The Gannochy Golf Club committee, led by their Captain, I. G. West, and their Secretary, Mr D. S. Ferguson, saw no particular reason why they should do this. Much fruitless though heated discussion ensued—to no avail. A subsequent suggestion by Mr

The 16th — Bunkers ahead.

I. G. West, captain of Gannochy Golf Club, that a match be held between th
two clubs was declined, on the grounds that 'No useful purpose would be met b
such a match and the matter should be dropped'.

When this present report was being prepared a senior member of the Gannc
chy Club who had been at the meeting was asked for his view of it. 'Weel' he saic
'When Tommy Marr became captain he tried to close doon the Gannochy ;
thegither. Aye, but he cudna'.' From this range that seems to be a pretty fai
assessment.

In the intervals of internecine strife the club found time to award full club
handicaps to some of its junior members. The junior section was run by Ro
Smith and some of his protégés were developing into outstanding golfers. Th
pick of that year's crop was Alastair Webster: handicap 3. Alastair then went o
to be Scottish Boys' Score Play Champion, a quarter-finalist in the British Boy
Championship and leader of the Scottish Boys' Team against England in tha
year.

In April 1975 the club suffered a tragic loss when W. F. Howe died. At th
committee meeting when the news was broken, Sandy Low, the Treasurer, pai
immediate tribute for all the help he had been given by the late hon. secretary an
said that though they had not always agreed, their differences had always ende
amicably.

A Tribute to Willie Howe

At the next A.G.M. the captain, Dr Marr, spoke of the sudden death of the honorary secretary, known to all affectionately as 'Willie'. He had been secretary of Edzell Golf Club for 16 years, his appointment having been in April 1959. He had the interests of the club at heart and many of the improvements to the clubhouse and the course were the result of his intense efforts. His lively presence would be missed for many a day. His tremendous enthusiasm was backed by an unflagging energy and his detailed organising ability was apparent in all he did for the club. This enthusiasm sometimes appeared to be somewhat brusque on occasion, but his own efforts were always 100 per cent and he expected the same from others.

The captain felt that something should be done by the club to commemorate Mr Howe, and asked members for suggestions. When all the suggested ideas of

The 16th looking back – No bunkers.

71

The 17th. Don't worry; he is left-handed.

competitions, cups, medals, salvers, mugs, named holes and mounted photographs had been considered, the decision was ultimately unanimous—put Willie's putter in a glass case in the men's lounge. One of the many outstanding features of Willie Howe was his putting. He seldom needed two. His expertise with the little old hickory-shafted prodder was legendary. As soon as the suggestion was made, everyone agreed that there could be no more fitting tribute. Willie's faithful putter is there to this day, mounted in a glass case in the men's bar. Look on it, you yippers, and despair. . . .

As a final token of gratitude, Mrs Hilda Howe was made an honorary life associate member of the club 'in appreciation of what her late husband and club secretary "Willie" had done for the club.' Mrs Howe herself had been of great service to the club in organising weekly bridge club meetings and similar gatherings.

There are many tales about Willie Howe in Edzell Golf Club and not many of them are apocryphal. Did he really have a path bulldozed through the whins at the 15th to accommodate his drive? Were the spaces between the front bunkers at the 3rd, 10th and 16th introduced to allow Willie's approach shot access to the green? Would the club have expended quite so much money, time and effort through Bob Inglis, Bob Hall, various greenkeeping firms and a persecuted green staff to provide the best greens in Scotland if Willie hadn't been a champion putter? You tell me. The one I do believe is that a man was once chased off the course by an irate Willie Howe for an act of gross indecency. He had his flannels tucked in to his socks, the swine. For another miscreant Willie kept a special file. Every misdemeanour and lapse of propriety by this particular individual was carefully listed and annotated. You fell foul of Willie at your peril.

One immediate and obvious change resulted from Willie's demise. The minute book ceased to bear his distinctive literary style with its abundance of Latin tags. *Pro tem, pro re nata, desideratum, ad hoc, et,* of course, *cetera,* peppered the immaculate structure of Willie's reports. It was no affectation, merely a reflection of the style of the time and an indication of the formality that has always graced Edzell Golf Club. Sic transit gloria Edzelli . . .

The history of a golf club must reflect the history of the age. A second-hand tractor bought for £440 in 1970 was sold again in 1976 for £500. The Club tie was replaced in 1976 because it was the wrong width and unfashionable. Kipper ties in Edzell Golf Club? Ken Cowie had four dozen left in his shop in Brechin and he approached the Club to take them off his hands before he would replace them. That's real history for you.

The year 1977 saw an increase in membership fees, keeping pace with the price of second-hand tractors. The new A class membership was set at £30, up from £20, and a joining fee of £20 was introduced. This was a period of roaring inflation and every item of club expenditure was increasing in multiples. The club was very fortunate just at this time in having Mr A. W. Low as treasurer. Not only did Sandy Low give an explicit account of current finance, he always offered an accurate prognosis of future costs. Sandy's reports as treasurer to the general meetings were paragons of their kind. Only by heeding Sandy Low's warnings did the club contrive at each general meeting to balance its income with ever increasing expenditure.

Staff Changes in the Seventies

With the untimely loss of W. F. Howe as secretary, the club was quite unprepared to find a replacement, and Captain W. J. R. Dawson stepped in to fill the gap. Bill Dawson is an army man to the core, or more accurately corps, and the members welcomed him as the ideal man to replace the secretary. W. J. R. Dawson was trained in administration; bright, cheery, immaculate in turnout and dedicated to the job. It seemed a fitting appointment. He was, however, only a stand-in. The new secretary was being groomed for stardom in the wings and Bill held the fort for a couple of years before handing over to R. C. Smith just before the new man became available.

'No, no,' says Bill Dawson, 'I'm not cut out for that kind of job.' 'There was one day when I was acting starter on the first tee and this member questioned my orders. If it had been in the Gordon barracks I'd have had him in the guardroom, feet not touching the ground, but you can't do that in a golf club—more's the pity—so I just packed it in.'

Just at this time the steward and his wife, Mr and Mrs Cowley, resigned, and when the question of appointing replacements arose, it was decided to incorporate a new steward's house into the proposed clubhouse alterations. The same meeting recorded the withdrawal of Edzell from the Strathmore League, and the reason seems particularly apposite to Edzell. The captain, Sandy Buchan, explained it at the general meeting:

> We had found ourselves rather out of step with other clubs taking part in the Strathmore League in that these clubs appeared to subsidise matches by meeting players' expenses, meals, etc., and also by making a contribution of £20 towards the end of season smoker and prize giving. This is completely against the traditions of Edzell where it has never been the practice that members not taking part in matches should be required to subsidise those who do. It has in fact always been the Edzell tradition that it was an honour and privilege to represent the club without being subsidised and the committee felt that they must withdraw from the competition.

There is the very essence of Edzell Golf Club in that statement. Sandy Buchan admirably expressed the ethos of the club when he said it. Edzell has always striven to maintain the Corinthian ideal.

The secretary-designate had now arrived in Edzell and was champing and jingling his bit ready for the off. In April 1977 he was loosed from his stall and started. The new man was W. H. W. Johnston.

W. H. W. (Willie) Johnston is the son of a Mearns farmer and was trained as a lad by the North of Scotland Bank in Inverbervie to do business largely with other Mearns farmers. A man born into such an environment and trained in such pursuits is a man eminently suited to be a golf club secretary—and well Edzell Golf Club knew it. Willie Johnston was worth waiting for. His happy personality and cheerful smile successfully mask the bank manager's nature. It has been said of Willie Johnston that he is like a beautiful flower. That flower, *mimosa sensitiva*, is the one that snaps shut and eats any unsuspecting insect that lands on it.

The arrival of Willie Johnston coincided with the redevelopment of the clubhouse and the building of the new steward's house. Bill floated happily through it all like a cork on a stormy sea. By 1978 the whole new unit was completed and the new stewards, Mr and Mrs Gibson, installed. Their tenure of office was brief as they resigned in 1979 and were succeeded by Mr and Mrs David Speed as club steward and caterer. The head greenkeeper, Bob Dickson, had also left to go to North Berwick and he was followed by Sam Watson.

An echo of a past clamour was heard in 1981 when the question of the state of the access bridge from the Glenesk Hotel was raised. This time the agreement was clearly enunciated. If the hotel wanted a bridge, the hotel could provide a bridge—subject to the approval and to the specification of the golf club. The hotel accepted the conditions and the bridge was rebuilt to the club's satisfaction.

Since the appointment of Captain E. C. Small in 1969, the tenure of office of the captain had been restricted to two years. Each subsequent captain had been appointed by general vote and on occasion the election had not been conducted entirely without acrimony. Different factions within the club would back different candidates—the Edzell group, the Brechin group, the farmers, the old gentlemen, the young upstarts—each would burrow away to undermine the others and it was obvious that this was not working in the best interests of the majority. The matter exercised the minds of the committee for a long time.

At the spring general meeting in 1980, under Captain David Hood, the whole thing was thrashed out and much heat generated. The proposed change was defined as:
On the retiral of the Captain, appointment of his successor will be by means of a sole nominee being selected by the committee and submitted to the spring general meeting, such sole nominee must, before nomination is submitted, be approached and agreement obtained of his willingness to serve as Club Captain.

This was immediately withdrawn in favour of an amendment proposed by David L. Cuthbert as follows:
Erase the words 'elected by the members of the Club' (in line 3) and insert after 'five other members' (line 6) 'The captain shall be elected by the committee. All other members of committee shall be elected by the members of the club.'

When almost everything that could be said on either side had been said, Sandy Buchan spoke up. With that pragmatism for which Sandy is renowned, he proposed 'no change'. A large majority supported him and the issue was closed:

temporarily. It is possible that the minds of the members at that particular meeting were concentrating on more pressing practicalities. A rise in bar prices had just been announced.

Whatever the system of selection, the meeting expressed total satisfaction with David Hood as captain and he was unanimously re-appointed. Dave left his mark on the course by donating ornamental trees and the evergreens behind the 11th tee and the 10th green which enhance that area considerably today. The condition of the course was now being praised highly by members and visitors alike, and the work of R. C. Smith, Green Convener, and his head greenkeeper, Sam Watson, were regularly commended at club meetings. Once again the club had the right man, Ron Smith, farmer of Broomfield and quondam fighter pilot, in the right job for the club.

This was a spell when the club seemed to glide smoothly on, its surface calm and unruffled. Under that surface, of course, the same currents that stir every golf club churned seismically. All the regular grievances were kept bubbling—the subscription, the method of appointing Captain, the price of drinks, the need for centrally heating the clubhouse, wear and tear of floor coverings, rabbits (four-legged), rabbits (two-legged), moles and other subversives. All these and a hantle more were subjected to the scrutiny of the bar-room analysts.

At the autumn meeting of 1981 the subscription for the next year was set at £55 for full membership with a £75 entrance fee. It kept creeping up. The new captain, Dr D. A. E. Mowat, was immediately involved with the problem of negotiating the course rent for the next five years. The proprietors had quoted a fair rent for the ground, based on its value as agricultural land, and considerably less than Kirriemuir, Barry and other clubs were paying. Most clubs would have accepted the figure and promptly paid up. Doc Mowat, in his lilting Caithness accent, politely requested a reduction.

It stands to the credit of Dalhousie Estates that they knocked £647 off the quoted figure and remained on good terms with the club. With his trusty bankers, Sandy Low and Willie Johnston backing him, Doctor Mowat was always going to be a hard man to deal with. His success in having the rent reduced was but a start. Doctor Mowat intended the club to buy the course and he set things in motion by sending another formal request to the Dalhousie trustees asking if there was any prospect of a sale and asking, further, that the club be informed if there was ever any likelihood of this. D. A. E. Mowat is not a man to be easily diverted from his chosen path, and his chosen path led directly to the purchase of the course.

At the spring meeting of 1982, after a series of spirited discussions on diverse topics with the exchange of some sharpish comments from the floor, there appeared under 'any other business', 'Ex-Captain Ewan Small remarked that of all the Edzell Golf Club meetings he had attended, this had been the most entertaining.' Dr D. A. E. Mowat was making his mark.

In July 1982 at a meeting of the captain and secretary with Mr J. C. L. Durant,

Factor to Dalhousie Estates, the first indication was given to the club that it might, possibly, buy the course.

From 15 to 21 August 1982, the British Girls' Open Amateur Championship was held at Edzell and the club was complimented and thanked for the efficiency with which the event was conducted. Claire White won the final 6 and 5 against Muriel Mackie, a Carnoustie lass. A refreshing insight into the working of Secretary W. H. W. Johnston's mind is revealed in his minute of the occasion: 'It was reported that apart from one or two who made complaints regularly, most members expressed approval . . . ' Willie had the members well summed up and he knew how to handle the 'one or two'.

Negotiations to buy the course were kept going by Dr Mowat. When things seemed to be slowing down he set up *ad hoc* committees to keep them going. Brigadier Oliver and Major T. P. Douglas Murray acted as intermediaries and a bout of elevated horse-trading ensued.

When Major T. P. Douglas Murray resigned as President in 1983, Brigadier J. A. Oliver, DSO, TD, DL, was appointed in his place. Major Murray had joined the Club in 1938, been Captain from 1956–65 and President since 1968. Brigadier Oliver had been a member since 1930 and his father had been one of the original members in 1895. The continuity of standards was being maintained despite an erosion of formality in the clubhouse dress rules which started just about then.

Dr D. A. E. Mowat was succeeded by Mr A. W. Low as captain and, on relinquishing office, Dr Mowat referred to the sterling service rendered by A. W. Low as treasurer to the club for thirteen years. Dr Mowat then invested him with a new captain's jewel which he was presenting to the club.

Purchasing the Course, 1983

When Dr Mowat ended his captaincy in April 1983, the negotiations for course purchase were still at a crucial stage but he was able to continue his involvement as a member of the *ad hoc* committee appointed to finalise the deal. There were some very fine points left to be settled—the inclusion of the greenkeeper's house, the definition of boundaries and titles, fishing and shooting rights adjoining the course, the ownership of trees, the naming of Edzell Golf Club trustees, the price. All these were debated and agreed. If the uninformed reader wonders if, in fact, such a transaction is any more complicated than buying a pound of sausages from one's local butcher, he need only read one paragraph from the 'Terms and Conditions' pertaining to the deal:

> There shall be exhibited prior to settlement a good marketable prescriptive progress of title. At settlement in exchange for payment of the said price there shall be delivered; (a) a valid and duly executed Disposition in favour of our clients or their nominees to which there will be annexed a plan showing the extent of the lands; (b) any prior writs falling to be delivered; (c) Interim Reports on the Searches hereinafter mentioned if not already supplied prior to settlement disclosing nothing prejudicial to our interest as purchasers; (d) a Letter of Obligation from your solicitors undertaking to deliver within twelve months of settlement Searches in the Property and Personal Registers brought down to the date of recording of the said Disposition and extending back not less than twenty years and five years respectively and showing clear records and nothing prejudicial to our clients' interest as purchasers.

That should inform him.

One of the most contentious issues of the whole exercise was the question of buying the greenkeeper's house—a formidable problem until the Dalhousie Trust solved it by including the house as part of the deal at no extra cost. There is no doubt that the final sum paid by Edzell Golf Club for the 132 acres of its course—and the Greenkeeper's house—was but a fraction of the true value. That sum, including VAT and postage, was £137,383.50—less than the price of a small suburban bungalow.

The question of buying the course had been complicated enough. The question of raising the money to pay for it had been worse. Every possible means of amassing enough cash to meet the deadline—bank loans, donations, higher fees, levies, sweepstakes and members' loans, had all been suggested and advocated by one group before being ridiculed and discarded by another. That group, in turn, would s. and a. their own scheme which in turn would be r. and d'd by the first. Only Willie Johnston was able to bring order into that chaos. With a few bank manager's observations, including a pertinent warning on the doubtful prudency of taking out a term loan of £50,000 which was going to cost £112,000 to repay, the matter was settled.

The money was raised by members' loans in multiples of £50 units at 5% interest to be repaid annually by ballot at the spring general meeting. A levy of £30 for 'A' class members and £20 for 'B' members would be imposed and the number of 'A' members would be increased. It all came right in the end and Edzell Golf Club now owns its own course. Willie's scheme for members' loans immediately raised £49,000 and the total was repaid within three years without any bank borrowing. Maybe the Bank regretted letting Willie go . . .

The amount of work put in by Willie Johnston and Sandy Low on financing the purchase of the course had been prodigious. Every member of the club showered thanks on them—and on Dr D. A. E. Mowat, the instigator of the project—but it was felt that the duties of secretary and treasurer had now become too onerous and time consuming for part-time volunteers. A more professional appointment of secretary/treasurer was envisaged and the post was advertised: on 1st March, 1984, James Hutchison was appointed: a most felicitous appointment.

At the spring general meeting of 1984 the Captain, A. W. Low, asked the members to stand in silent tribute to Mrs Jim Webster who had died, tragically, as the result of a recent car accident. Mrs Webster, 'Chatt' to all in Edzell Golf Club, was Jim's wife and constant helpmeet; a most popular figure in the club and renowned for her cheerful outlook and happy personality. On countless occasions Chatt had helped out in the Clubhouse whenever help was needed and her usual presence in Jim's shop made it a pleasure to do business there.

At a subsequent meeting it was decided to institute the Chatt Webster Memorial Trophy Competition and this is now one of the best supported events in the club calendar. Chatt Webster continues to be sorely missed by everyone who knew her.

With the clamour about buying the course now stilled, the main topic of conversation in the men's bar soon became focused on the pressing need for the clubhouse renovation. When visitors remarked on the 'olde worlde charm' and 'traditional ambience' of the place, it began to dawn on even the most dedicated antiquarian member that maybe there was just a hint of criticism in the comment. Spike-scarred wooden bench seats, tread-worn floorboards, out-dated cast iron coat-pegs and a general air of shabby-genteel dilapidation had become the hallmarks of Edzell Golf Club in the 1980s. The changing rooms were microcosms of 1920s sophistication. Intermittent refurbishing over the years had done little to eradicate the stamp of the original 1925 décor. With that cautious procrastination which is another of the club's hallmarks, the matter of refurbishing the clubhouse was discussed.

It was the spring general meeting of 23rd March, 1988, before a scheme of re-development for the clubhouse was finally adopted and passed for action. Work was scheduled to start on 1 November, 1988. Before these decisions were made there had been a welter of argument and discussion amongst the members. That is how a good golf club works. The roof had to be re-tiled; that was certain. What else should be done? Build a new clubhouse? Leave the building as it was but refurbish the interior? Build on to the present clubhouse? Shoot the captain? The captain was Ian Sutherland and no man could be less deserving of such a fate. It was assumed that the last suggestion was no more than a *cri de coeur* against officialdom in general. As an indication of the value of J. T. Sutherland as captain, one has only to refer to his address to that spring meeting. *Inter alia*, he referred to the increasing importance of leisure activities, including golf, and the need to prepare for the ever growing demand for facilities. He stressed the need for the club to be prudent in its planning for the future and continued:

> As Edzell members, we are in the enviable position of owning our course and clubhouse, of being unburdened by debt and seeing our way clearly forward to profitable years, as Jim Hutchison has so clearly exhibited to us this evening. The ball is at our feet.

Whilst the golfing purist might ponder the significance of the last sentence, that is a statement of the most judicious intent. Ian Sutherland saw the way ahead and was set to follow it. A redeveloped clubhouse represented the first step along that way.

Captains and Committee Men

Whilst all these momentous decisions were being made by succeeding captains, the rank and file committee men continued with their more mundane tasks. At one meeting it was remarked that the auditor, Mr Booth, had been auditing the club's books for about a century without any proper recompense. It was stated, further, that Mr Booth had declined to accept an increase in the honorarium about twenty-five years ago and had said only the other day, when asked, that the sum was quite adequate. This time the committee decided that it would insist and added £25 to the meagre annual sum. In his letter of thanks, Mr Booth enclosed a cheque for £50 as a donation to the club's funds. There you have it. The spirit of Edzell Golf Club, incarnate: Fred Booth.

Another of the club's most valued officials, Gordon Baxter, the senior's secretary, tragically died in 1988. Gordon was the friendliest of men and a most popular figure in the club. His passing was a shock and a sorrow to all his friends.

When J. T. Sutherland vacated the captaincy, having set the clubhouse development scheme in motion, Dr A. R. Lyall proposed a vote of thanks and mentioned particularly 'the way he had most expeditiously and professionally chaired the meetings, both Committee and General.' This was most certainly the case. Ian Sutherland's meetings were classic examples of business efficiency. He was a golfer as well. He won the V. and A. Vase of the Royal and Ancient of St Andrews twice in consecutive years—a feat done only once previously.

J. T. Sutherland's term of office was a period of particular harmony for the club. 'Ian' Sutherland is a man of quiet, good nature and his skill as captain was to transmit these personal qualities to his fellows. Whilst all Edzell Golf Club captains are, of course, gentlemen, it must be said of Ian Sutherland that he was, clearly, *primus inter pares*. During his time as captain the club enjoyed a cruise through untroubled waters steered safely on course by the sure hand of Ian Sutherland—even when he had to jury-rig the tiller.

J. T. Sutherland's successor, T. F. Inglis, inherited the plans for the refurbishment of the clubhouse. This was the next major task for the club, and Tom Inglis's successful direction of that project occupied most of his energies during his time of office.

When any golf club captain is appointed, he comes to the job only after having undergone a long slog through the ranks of sub-committees and convenerships. He comes trained in the ways of his particular club, but if he is to become a good

March, 1993. *Left to right*: J. B. Webster, A. W. Low, W. W. Low, A. J. Webster.

captain he comes also with a dedication, an inner resolution, to put his personal stamp on the place. It is perhaps unfortunate that the present, two-year, stint of the Edzell captain generally precludes his realising any such ambition. The demands of finance and the dictates of routine maintenance usually confine the captain to a limited role. In Tom Inglis's case, that role was to see to the clubhouse, but how much Tom did with the course is sometimes overlooked and how much more he would have done had the clubhouse not intruded to divert him from his real interest in the club, is missed. Tom Inglis is a retired farmer—if a farmer can ever retire—and a round of golf in Edzell with Tom Inglis is as much a nature ramble as a round of golf. He studies the course, he studies the trees, he comments on past, present and future developments. As the brother of past Captain Robert Inglis who did so much to develop the course and a past green convener himself, Tom Inglis keeps Edzell Golf Club in the forefront of his interests. His stewardship was one of the more constructive in the Club's history.

One of the important changes which took place during Tom Inglis's captaincy was the retiral of Jim Webster. For 26 years Jim had served Edzell Golf Club far beyond the bounds of his obligation. Jim was always there with a quiet word of support and encouragement to the club golfer. His lessons were reasoned suggestions, his advice was kind. Before turning professional golfer, Jim was a precision engineer and this was evident in the work he did on members' equipment.

Jim Webster used to take in dilapidated pieces of golf tackle—articles that any other pro. would have politely declined to handle—and rebuild them. With only basic facilities and using only hand tools, Jim would carefully reshape and repair battered old items that would have been accepted more readily by a Sotheby's sale of antique golfing memorabilia. It is in the nature of golfers to grow attached to certain clubs, and Jim spent long hours rebuilding favoured drivers and putters that might more reasonably have graced the walls of a golf museum. It was Jim's basic good nature that let him do it. In all his work for Edzell Golf Club, Jim had been fully supported by his family, and when he retired the committee had had the good sense to appoint his son Alastair in his place. Alastair is now a worthy replacement for Jim, and Edzell Golf Club is again becoming internationally known because of his prowess.

In his address at the 1990 autumn meeting, Captain Inglis was able to list recent achievements of the Club which put the members in a very favourable position for the future. He cited:

Purchase of the Course 7 years ago	£132,000
Installation of a new Sprinkler system	30,000
Renewal of Course Machinery	40,000
Phase 1 Clubhouse Improvements	62,000
Extension of Car Park	18,000
	£282,000

'This is a considerable achievement of which the Club members should be rightfully proud and which stands the club in good stead whatever the view held.'

When Tom Inglis said that, he highlighted the fact that the present system of tenure for Edzell Golf Club captains does make for continuity. The responsibility for any development on course or clubhouse is dispersed over several captaincies. Two years is seldom enough time for any major scheme to be conceived, adopted, set going and completed, so that a succession of executives will share the responsibilities. So much for permanent Captains . . .

The continuity of Tom Inglis's reign was maintained by Dr A. R. Lyall, a much respected figure. It is probable that a lifetime of listening to the complaints of patients and ministering to the needs of the sick had schooled Dr Lyall admirably for the role of Edzell Golf Club Captain. He certainly had his quota of complaints during his term and he dealt with them all quietly and efficiently. The tone of Dr Lyall's captaincy was one of quiet confidence. Where other men might have flown off handles, Dr Lyall's reaction was always diplomatic and dignified. It quite surprised Edzell Golf Club and positively transformed Bert Scott.

A Retrospective Glance: The Dawn of the Centenary

With the centenary year now dawning, a retrospective glance over the shoulder of the years confirms the fact that the club is in good order today. There can never be a time in any golf club's history when everything is deemed to be perfect, of course. Such a club would be well on the way to moribundity. There must be members at Edzell today who complain—Willie Johnston referred to them as 'the one or two who made complaints regularly'. It is the complainers in any group who overcome the inertia of the majority and activate acceptable reform. Conflict of interest is bound to arise between the young players and the old players in any golf club. The nature of the game ensures it. Young, fit, players will look for long untrammelled space in which to fire long untrammelled drives whilst the old men will seek craftily achievable targets within their limited three-stroke range. It is all part of the eternal tussle between youth and age. The young in any healthy society must rebel just as surely as the old must counter that rebellion. Only by such counterpoise action is a balance maintained. That is exactly why you young upstarts in Edzell Golf Club today can lay off the agitprop and keep quiet for a bit. Leave the rest of the medal tees where they are, confound you!

The ladies' section of Edzell Golf Club exists as a model to other ladies' golf clubs. The relationship with the parent club is always one of happy co-operation. M. Nicholas Chauvin would have found no occasion to criticise the Edzell Ladies and no hint of chauvinism arises. Over the years the husbands of Edzell lady golfers have ensured that their spouses' interests were well cared for; the ladies have benefited and harmony has prevailed. Even the most dedicated feminist would shrink from sharing the same tees, handicaps, competitions and toilet facilities as the men. The feeling is mutual.

One of the more obvious reflections of the accord that exists between the Ladies' and Mens' Club of Edzell—apart from the pride taken in Nancy Duncan's successes—is the tremendous contribution of Mrs Anne Donald to the corporate image of the club. It is Mrs Donald who is responsible for the strikingly attractive heath and heather rockery. It is Mrs Donald—'Annie' to every member—who is responsible for the beautiful flower decorations in the clubhouse. Annie Donald is an artist, a creative artist, who has the eye and the hand to provide stimulating yet soothing flower arrangements crafted to calm the fevered minds of golfers. For golfers are chiels whose minds are gey often fevered. They arrive in anticipatory dread, they perform under Sisyphean stress, they grieve inconsolably in retrospective gloom. Little wonder then that the therapeutic effect of Annie's flower power is so valuable. The fact that, by profession, Annie is one of the anaesthetists at Stracathro Hospital may not be entirely insignificant in this context.

The course at Edzell is regularly monitored. Since the Hawtree Report was mainly implemented by 1974, their man, John Soutar, has kept up regular visits to supervise progress. Successive green conveners have heard his advice. To what extent that advice has been heeded one can see from the state of the course today. It is in grand nick. John Soutar's visits have now terminated and the result of his work is evidenced in smooth fairways, velvet greens, amiable bunkers—bar that little divil left front of the third green, and I don't think we can blame John Soutar for that—and a generally delightful course.

When one considers the unbearable weight of abuse that is daily heaped on the head of every serving green convener, it is a marvel that any man can ever be prevailed upon to accept the post. The present incumbent, Willie Watson, is a man made for the job. A timber merchant to trade, Willie is a man dedicated to the countryside, to trees, to woods and to work. When his green staff has been under pressure Willie has cut the fairways and cleaned the car park himself. Willie leads by example. In any ballot for 'most popular Edzell member' Willie would rate highly and his prospects would not be diminished one jot by his habit, when playing for the Seniors, of leaving a full flask of sloe gin on the tenth tee for the next lot following on.

That the high standards set by the Hon. C. M. Ramsay and the Rev. T. C. Sturrock in 1895 are being maintained in Edzell today, one has only to think of the Club Championship Final of 1993 when Gary Tough and Billy Taylor contested a memorable match. Spectators who followed them that day saw the two lads play a needle match when Bill won the first half and Gary won the second and the match. That match was played in a spirit of genuine friendship and a mood of mutual congratulation. They gave us an example of the finest sportsmanship anyone could wish for—in any sport. The fact that there had to be a winner was incidental to the pleasure they provided. That is the standard of Edzell golf and the club is proud to have such players in its ranks.

That it will continue to produce such members is ensured by Jim Adamson, for Jim now runs the junior section. Coached in technique by Alastair Webster and his excellent assistant, John Logue, since the untimely death of Jim Webster, the juniors are again well catered for. Alastair has an International reputation as a coach and John Logue is a very competent assistant pro. and a first-rate example to the youngsters. To back up the coaching, Jim Adamson can concentrate on etiquette. No breach of good golfing form is tolerated by either coach, and every aspect and detail of the game is covered. Edzell juniors have always been fortunate in their schooling, for Jim Adamson follows the line of Bob Hall, Ron Smith and Willie Johnston. The line is practically biblical in its listing of respected elders.

Prominent in any such list of respected Edzell elders would be the name of Alan White; a man of prodigious industry and happy disposition. Alan's effervescent personality and ever-ready smile enable him to organise the seniors' inter-Club matches with total acceptance. And that takes some doing.

Way back when the Edzell folk first heard rumours of the proposed new golf club, their reaction was one of fear that the 'Brechin nobs' were about to take over. It is a reassuring fact that no such eventuality has occurred. The point was emphasised to a club member on his own one day when he caught up on the couple in front. He was politely invited to join the two and play together from the 15th.

When the last four holes had been played, in a spirit of good-humoured mediocrity, and the group came off the 18th green, they shook hands and said their thanks. The lone golfer made his way into the clubhouse and met one of the older members coming out.

'D'ye ken fa that wis ye wis playin' wi'?' enquired the older member.

'No,' said the lone golfer.

'The King o'Denmark,' said the older member. 'He's a member.'

With all social barriers eliminated, the Clubhouse renovated, the course in classic condition, William Low's monument—the big shed—completed and Captain John Adams steering the club through its calmest water ever, it would seem that all is well with Edzell Golf Club. Our founding fathers can rest in peace, for the future of the club looks to be assured. When the course was bought in 1983, the members had contributed £49,000 under the members' loan scheme and the total was repaid within three years without any bank borrowing. That was the strength of the club then and with lawyer William Low and businessman John Adams as captains for the past four years, the combination of entrepreneurial initiative and jurisprudent circumspection has been continued. Entrepreneurial initiative and jurisprudent circumspection? You can't do much better than that.

One must not be too sanguine, of course. The members continue to murmur complaints. The captain comes to office charged with creative energy and leaves with the current workload uncompleted. The committee strives to accommodate every demand and usually succeeds in alienating no more than half the members at best. Such a club is an active and successful club.

Much of the harmony that does prevail in Edzell right now is directly due to the club's present employees. The green staff under the mercurial Sam regularly accomplish their herculean tasks, the catering staff cater enterprisingly, the bar staff continue to provide paramedic prescriptions for golf-shocked patients. The club is in as good heart as any club.

It is also in good hands—a particularly safe pair of hands. The secretary, Jim Hutchison, backed by his able, efficient and utterly charming assistant, Maureen Smith, is well on the way to ranking with Willie Howe in the history of Edzell Golf Club. Less abrasive than Willie—more diplomat than bruiser—Jim Hutchison has all the skills of committee management that your good secretary must command. A committee meeting organised by Jim Hutchison is a committee meeting that will proceed smoothly and efficiently through its agenda. What that committee may not realise is the volume of work performed by Jim Hutchison in preparation for that meeting. Jim Hutchison is one of these invaluable citizens whose only hobby is his work. That may explain in part his handicap of 24. It certainly explains why, at the autumn meeting of '93, the company responded so enthusiastically to Dr Mowat's spontaneous call for a vote of thanks to Mr J. M. Hutchison.

The history of Edzell Golf Club is the story of its past. That is a pity. It bars the historian from writing more fully about its present—or what a history that would be! Members who gather lost balls like old ale gathers wasps: members who coach their opponents to destruction: members—can there be any such in Edzell?—who throw clubs and kick bags.

There are such members in every golf club, known to their fellows and quite oblivious of their own sins. Such individuals are the stuff of society. On Edzell golf course on any reasonably clear day one may expect to encounter the teacher whose arithmetic is such that he consistently counts one under but has never, ever, been known to count one over. The professional man whose diagnosis, after a duffed drive, is couched in such lancet language as would have him debarred by the Union of Billingsgate Fish Porters, and the former Supervisor of Parks, Playing Fields, Cemeteries and Open Spaces who drove the buggy right over the ball-washer at the fourth tee and wrecked it, with no shred of an excuse. Think what a golfer's tale that lot could furnish!

The game of Golf itself could serve to illustrate the futility of all human endeavour. The topped drive, the missed putt, the shank. Life is but a pale shadow of golf. Go into the men's bar of Edzell Golf Club any day and savour the scene. They play a lot of their golf in there. Each little table has its speaker and the air is full of golf:

'I knew as soon as I hit it I should have taken a seven iron.'

'I put it straight for the left lip and it screwed past on the right. That eighth green is a disgrace.'

'Did you see my second at the sixteenth when the wind put it in the bunker?'

'I would have won but . . . ' but nobody is listening.

That is the essence of all golfing conversation in all men's bars all over the land. The speakers are ridding themselves of stress, tension and a deeply subconscious sense of guilt. The others are merely waiting their turn. Psychiatrists can charge three figures for the same service—and they need listen only perfunctorily. Golf provides the great escape from whatever it is one is trying to escape from. Golfers emerge from their clubhouses after a round, refined and restored, purged and cleansed from physical ordeal and spiritual torment. Golf is the great prophylactic.

As he looks out from the clubhouse over the verdant mantle of the course today Captain John Adams must feel honoured. To be captain of such a club at such a time must be deeply satisfying. A club that owns its own course and clubhouse, its own grounds, woods, properties and shop. A club where members meet as friends and equals—where kings and commoners can commingle—must sustain a happy and contented captain. When he steps on to that first hallowed tee his feelings must be buoyant with optimism. He bears the honour of his position and the promise of his game. Let's just hope he responds and knocks another .2 off.

EDZELL GOLF CLUB CHAMPIONS

1907	J. Duncan	1946	L. W. Garland
1908	C. Ferrier	1947	G. Crighton
1909	F. M. Richardson	1948	N. F. Taylor
1910	A. N. S. Sandeman	1949	J. B. Webster
1911	C. E. Gilroy	1950	J. B. Webster
1912	C. E. Gilroy	1951	J. B. Webster
1913	—	1952	J. B. Webster
1914	E. S. Kennedy	1953	D. S. Ferguson
1915–18	No competition	1954	J. B. Webster
1919	A. G. Gowans	1955	J. B. Webster
1920	A. F. M. Guild	1956	J. B. Webster
1921	J. McIntyre	1957	A. D. Robertson
1922	G. B. Smart	1958	C. B. Webster
1923	C. Ferrier	1959	A. D. Robertson
1924	C. Ferrier	1960	C. B. Webster
1925	J. C. Jessop	1961	J. B. Webster
1926	J. C. Jessop ⎱ Tie C. Ferrier ⎰	1962	G. Crighton
		1963	D. W. Ferguson
1927	A. F. M. Guild	1964	D. W. Ferguson
1928	J. McIntyre	1965	D. W. Ferguson
1929	C. Ferrier	1966	J. H. Fairweather
1930	C. Ferrier	1967	B. W. Beattie
1931	J. C. Jessop	1968	D. W. Ferguson
1932	J. McIntyre	1969	D. W. Ferguson
1933	G. A. McKenzie	1970	B. W. Beattie
1934	E. C. Small	1971	J. A. Abbot
1935	W. Gellatly ⎱ W. Manson ⎰ Tie	1972	J. K. A. Bruce
		1973	D. W. Ferguson
1936	W. Gellatly ⎱ W. Manson ⎰	1974	R. Thomson
		1975	A. J. Webster
1937	A. N. MacCullie	1976	A. J. Webster
1938	H. A. Garvie	1977	G. W. Paton
1939	A. N. MacCullie	1978	A. J. Webster
1940–45	No competiton	1979	J. K. A. Bruce

1980	J. K. A. Bruce	1988	J. K. A. Bruce
1981	I. R. Kerr	1989	I. G. T. Farquhar
1982	A. J. Renilson	1990	G. W. Tough
1983	W. Taylor	1991	W. Taylor
1984	W. Taylor	1992	W. Taylor
1985	G. W. Tough	1993	G. W. Tough
1986	J. K. A. Bruce	1994	G. W. Tough
1987	W. Taylor		

EDZELL GOLF CLUB CAPTAINS

1895–98	The Hon. C. M. Ramsay	1956–64	T. P. D. Murray, Esq.
1899–1900	Patrick Chalmers, Esq.	1965–68	J. A. Ogg, Esq.
1901	John Shiell, Esq.	1969–70	E. C. Small, Esq.
1902–03	W. Shaw Adamson, Esq.	1971–72	A. J. Hunter, Esq.
1904–18	The Rt. Hon. The Earl of Dalhousie	1973–74	Dr. T. C. K. Marr
		1975–76	R. Inglis, Esq.
1919–20	Patrick Chalmers, Esq.	1977–78	Alexander Buchan, Esq.
1921	A. G. Gowans, Esq.	1979–80	David Hood, Esq.
1922–29	Sam Edwards, Esq.	1981–82	Dr. D. A. E. Mowat
1930–32	T. Maule Guthrie, Esq.	1983–84	A. W. Low, Esq.
1933–36	F. A. Ferguson, Esq.	1985–86	Wm. H. W. Johnston, Esq.
1937–38	John Hunter, Esq.	1987–88	J. T. Sutherland, Esq.
1939–45	T. M. Wood, Esq.	1989–90	T. F. Inglis, Esq.
1946–47	C. Gordon Mackie, Esq.	1991–92	Dr. A. R. Lyall
1948–52	N. J. H. Goodchild, Esq.	1993–95	W. W. Low, Esq.
1953–55	Capt. R. G. Duke, R.N.	1995–	J. E. Adams, Esq.

Index